Lies, Lies and More Lies

Lies, Lies and More Lies

The Campaign To Defame Hindu/Indian Nationalism

Vivek

iUniverse, Inc.
New York Lincoln Shanghai

Lies, Lies and More Lies
The Campaign To Defame Hindu/Indian Nationalism

iUniverse books may be ordered through booksellers or by contacting:

iUniverse
2021 Pine Lake Road, Suite 100
Lincoln, NE 68512
www.iuniverse.com
1-800-Authors (1-800-288-4677)

Library of Congress Control Number: 2007904121

ISBN: 978-0-595-43549-4 (pbk)
ISBN: 978-0-595-87876-5 (ebk)

Printed in the United States of America

Dedicated to the 5,000-year-old Hindu civilization that is the basis of the modern, secular, democratic, and pluralistic state of India that was reborn in 1947

If you tell a lie big enough and keep repeating it, people will eventually come to believe it.

—Joseph Goebbels, Nazi Minister for Propaganda

Even if I am a minority of one, the truth is still the truth.

—Mahatma Gandhi

Truth alone will endure; all the rest will be swept away before the tide of time.

—Mahatma Gandhi

About the Cover

The Lion Capital of Emperor Ashoka of the Mauryan dynasty forms the centerpiece of the cover. The Lion Capital was installed in the third century B.C. at Sarnath to mark the site from where Buddha proclaimed his message of peace and goodwill to the world. Modern India adopted this emblem to reaffirm its commitment to these principles.

The motif itself consists of four lions, symbolizing power, courage, and confidence, standing back to back. The lions rest on a circular abacus girdled by four smaller animals guarding the four directions: the lion on the north, the horse to the south, the elephant to the east, and the bull on the west. Beneath the abacus is a lotus in full bloom denoting life and creativity. Etched below are the words, *Satyameva Jayate* (in Devanagari script) derived from the *Mundaka Upanishad*, meaning "Truth alone Triumphs."

The saffron band at the top and green at the bottom depict the colors of the Indian National flag.

Contents

Preface... xv

Part One: The Genesis

1   Introduction... 3

    1a   Who are the Nazis?.................................... 12

2   Naipaul's India: "The Hindu Land is a Wounded
Civilization" 15

3   India as an Entity 21

4   Controversy about History 29

5   Truth in History: Destruction of Hindu Temples ... 34

6   Changing Demography of South Asia 42

Part Two: Kashmir

7   The Kashmir Dispute: A Different Perspective 57

8   Kashmiri Pandits: Ethnic Cleansing the World does
Not See 63

9   Amarnath: A Lesson in Secularism....................... 70

10 A Hindu CM for J&K: Any Takers? 74

Part Three: Contemporary India

11 Lies, Lies, and More Lies 79

12 The Babri Masjid Controversy............................. 85

13 Hindu Anger 86

14 Godhra and its Aftermath: A Dispassionate View 90

15 Hindu Temples in the Age of Pseudo-Secularism 96

16 Indian Intellectuals: A Failure to Lead 100

17 The Miracle that is India 104

18 Freedom of Religion and Conversion Not
    Synonymous 111

19 The Sachar Report: An Objective Analysis............................. 116

20 Hope and Reality 122

21 India: The Need for a New Secularism 125

22 Note of Caution 133

Glossary 135

Notes and References 137

Maps

Map 1: Political Map of India xvii

Map 2: India during the Mauryan Empire (250 B.C.)..................... 22

Map 3: Boundaries of Modern India(not to scale).......................... 23

Map 4: Europe in A.D. 1 26

Map 5: British India 27

Preface

It was the welcome dinner at a downtown Boston restaurant. The next day would begin a rigorous two-year course that would land a group of middle-aged professionals a degree in health management. So here we were, the previous night, gathered around the dinner table, making small talk and getting to know each other. The topic veered around to current events and one of the professors made an off-the-cuff, deprecating remark about Hindu fundamentalism. This was a man who I would come to know later as a man of extraordinary intellect and knowledge and probably one of the best teachers I have ever come across. However, his remarks that night indicated to me the depth of unawareness that exists among even the learned population of the West with regards to *Hindutva* (Hindu Nationalism). Hence this book.

To one unfamiliar with India, it is very easy to confuse *Hindutva* with Hindu fundamentalism, for there is no word in the English language that can truly describe this abstract notion. *Hindutva* is an ideology that took root among the Hindus of India in the early part of the twentieth century and gradually progressed over the years to become the dominant political force in India by the turn of the century. Its genesis lay in the thousand years of foreign subjugation, exploitation, and suppression that preceded it. And today it remains the sole bulwark against the spreading Islamic fundamentalism in South Asia.

I have often been confronted with the question: "Does a billion-strong community really need protection?" The answer is yes. Although it may seem paradoxical on the face of it, I hope that by the end of the book this statement will become more plausible.

How did I come to believe in *Hindutva*? Indoctrination is a word that easily springs to one's mind. But that is not so. I grew up in a totally apolitical environment. My father was a government official who rarely spoke about politics and my mother a religious housewife. My belief stems from the little day-to-day incidents that occurred in my life, the current events that unfolded before my eyes, and my reading of Indian history, despite the fact that the history books of my time glorified Islamic rule and colonial invasion and made it appear that they were the best things that happened to India. From my school days to the present time, my belief has grown stronger and stronger. It was and remains to this day an independent, objective assessment made by a young boy with a virgin mind.

Why did I want to publish this collection of articles? For two reasons. One, I could not voice my opinion through the usual channels and I wanted to convey my message to a wider audience. The English-language media in India, for the greater part of the last 50 years, have been in the clutches of a cabal of editors who harbor an irrational, pathological aversion to *Hindutva* and who make sure that articles like mine never see the light of day, despite being objective. The articles in this book express my reaction to some current events or comment on some aspects of Indian history.

Second, through this series of articles I hope to make people understand what *Hindutva* stands for and what it really means. I did not want this book to be a long, dreary treatise; I have kept it simple and concise so that it is readable.

One last word. Truth and honesty must form the basis of any ideology. I have made every attempt to ensure the authenticity of my writings. Despite that, I am open to correction if anyone can locate any factual errors in the book.

March 29, 2007   Vivek

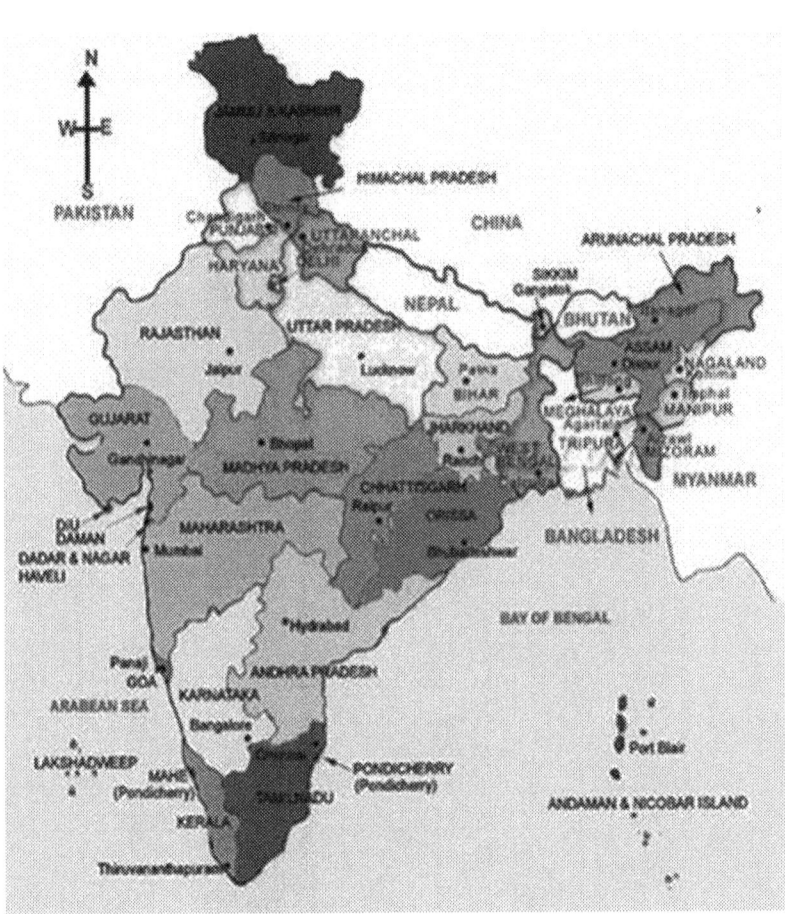

Map 1: Political Map of India

Basic Facts

Official Name: Bharat (Hindi); Republic of India (English)

Independence: August 15, 1947 (from British colonial rule)

Type of Government: Sovereign Socialist Democratic Republic with a Parliamentary system of Government

Capital: New Delhi

Population: 1,028,610,328 (2001 Census)

Area: 3.3 million sq. km

Location: Lies between latitudes 8° 4' and 37° 6' North, and longitudes 68° 7' and 97° 25' East

States: Comprises 29 States and 6 Union Territories

Length of Coastline: 7,600 km

Languages: National language is Hindi. Official business conducted in English. The Indian Constitution also officially recognizes 22 regional languages.

Major Religions: Hinduism (80.5%), Islam (13.4%), Christianity (2.3%), Buddhism (0.8%), Sikhism (1.9%), Others (1.1%).

Literacy: 64.8%

Political Parties: Bharatiya Janata Party (BJP), Indian National Congress, Communist Party of India (CPI), Communist Party of India–Marxist (CPM)

President: A. P. J. Abdul Kalam

Prime Minister: Dr Manmohan Singh

National Anthem: *"Jan gana mana"* written by Rabindranath Tagore

National Song: "*Vande Mataram*" composed in Sanskrit by
                        Bankimchandra Chatterji
National Emblem: Replica of the Lion Capital of Sarnath
National Flag: Horizontal tricolor in equal proportions of
                        deep saffron on the top, white in the middle,
                        and dark green at the bottom, with a wheel in
                        navy blue in the center of the white band.
National Animal: Tiger (*Panthera tigris*)
National Bird: Peacock
National Flower: Lotus
National Tree: Banyan
National Fruit: Mango
National Currency: Rupee (One rupee = 100 paise)
National Sport: Hockey

Part One

The Genesis

The loss of the past meant the loss of that civilisation, the loss of a fundamental idea of India, and the loss therefore to a nationalist-minded man, of a motive for action. It was a part of the feeling of purposelessness of which many Indians spoke.

—V. S. Naipaul, *A Wounded Civilization*

1

Introduction

Ignorance and malicious deception have contributed to making *Hindutva* (Hindu Nationalism) a much misunderstood and much maligned ideology. Often terms like militancy and fundamentalism are used in association with this movement. Nothing can be further from the truth.

Hindutva defies precise definition especially in an alien language like English. People have tried to define it in several ways. Some claim that it is a combination of "Hindu" and *tattva* (principles). The closest description of *Hindutva* in English would be "Hindu-ness." To me it is a feeling; a state of mind that has evolved from a deep sense of hurt and one which seeks dignity and justice with civilized assertiveness. It is a statement against foreign invasion. Simply put, it is a firm stand against oppression, evil, and injustice.

Origin

While the term *Hindutva* was coined by Veer Savarkar, a Hindu nationalist and freedom fighter (against British colonialism) in the 1920s in response to Muslim extremism, the concept of a need for Hindu assertiveness dates back to the times of Shivaji. Shivaji was a seventeenth-century Hindu chieftain from central India who repulsed the tyrannical Islamic Mughal rule and restored Hindu primacy to the greater part of India.

Indian history from the seventh century onwards till the twentieth century has been one long, tragic story of repeated foreign invasions, inhumane butchery of millions of innocent Hindus, senseless destruction of hundreds of Hindu temples, and economic devastation that reduced one of the richest countries in the world to unimaginable penury. Islamic invaders who reached India's borders in the seventh century A.D. gave a new meaning and a new dimension to the words destruction, loot, repression, and human carnage.

The brutalities of this era are clearly corroborated by world historians and are not the fantasies of Hindu nationalists as some in India claim. Alain Danielou in *Histoire de l'Inde* writes:

> From the time Muslims started arriving, around A.D. 632, the history of India becomes a long, monotonous series of murders, massacres, spoilations, destructions. It is, as usual, in the name of "a holy war" of their faith, of their sole God, that the barbarians have destroyed civilisations, wiped out entire races.[1]

American historian Will Durant in *The Story of Civilization* categorically states that the Islamic conquest of India is "*probably the bloodiest story in history*"[emphasis mine]. He adds: "It is a discouraging tale, for its evident moral is that civilization is a precarious thing, whose delicate complex of order and liberty, culture and peace may at any time be overthrown by barbarians invading from without...."[2]

More recently Francois Gautier, the India correspondent for the French newspaper *Le Figaro* has this to say about the Muslim invasion in his book *Rewriting Indian History*.

> Let it be said right away: the massacres perpetrated by Muslims in India are unparalleled in history, bigger than the holocaust of the Jews by the Nazis; or the massacre of the Armenians by the Turks; more extensive even than the slaughter of the South American native populations by the invading Spanish and Portuguese.[3]

It was in this setting that the ideology of *Hindutva* began taking shape. I would have considered it perverse had such all-consuming evil evoked no resistance or response from the Hindus. I would have considered the Hindus effete had they not rebelled against this injustice. It rankles me even today when people try to gloss over these atrocities or attempt to mitigate the magnitude of these crimes.

I am willing to forgive, but *I am not willing to forget.* For to forget is to leave the door open for these atrocities to recur. Subsequent exploitation by the British further helped to strengthen this suspicion of foreigners and their motives. Independence from the British in 1947 held forth a lot of promise for the Hindu: at last, almost one thousand years of subjugation was coming to an end. Little did he realize that he would continue to be at the receiving end (see the chapter "Hindu Anger") as a result of a warped philosophy of Nehruvian secularism, which was the result of the fear of Nazism and an ignorance of *Hindutva.*

Nehruvian Secularism

This secularism that was promoted in independent India did not subscribe to the dictionary meaning of the term (as the articles in this book will indicate). It was a corruption that was thrust upon the Indian people by Machiavellian machinations that involved fraud, deceit, and obfuscation. The key mechanisms in this evil endeavor took the form of:

1) Destruction of the Hindu identity by distorting history

   a. That India never existed as a single entity

   b. That the Islamic invasion was a golden period and did not involve the massive destruction of temples or massacre of millions of Hindus

2) Creating dissension in Hindu Society

   a. North-South Divide: Aryan-Dravidian theory

   b. Exploitation of the caste differences in Hindu society

3) Raising the specter of Nazism by labeling it a hate philosophy

Ironically, those who leveled the charges of Nazism against the *Hindutva* movement were themselves guilty of using Goebbelesque techniques to further their ends (read "Who are the Nazis?").

Not a Hate Rant

When one views *Hindutva* against this background, one realizes it is not about superiority. By no means is it a hate rant. Neither is it poetry of love. Rather, it is a pragmatism that is destined to confer on the Hindu his lost sense of pride and ensure the protection of his interests. It is the agonizing cry for justice and dignity of a people long suppressed and tortured; a cry that embodies the agony of the past and a new-found confidence of the present which together hopes to ensure a secure future.

That it is not directed against other religions was made clear even by Savarkar (denigrated as the epitome of hatred) in his thesis.

> Therefore even from the point of Indian nationality, must ye, O Hindus, consolidate and strengthen Hindu nationality; *not to give wanton offence to any of our non-Hindu compatriots*, in fact to any one in the world but in just and urgent defence of our race and land; to render it impossible for others to betray her to or subject her to unprovoked attack by any of those "Pan-isms" that are struggling forth from continent to continent.[4]

The early 1900s were not an age of political correctness and one could have got away with anything one wished to say. The fact that Savarkar expressly underlines his commitment not to offend others is a clear indication that it was not hate that spawned this philosophy. To oppose foreign invasion, to oppose suppression of people is the moral duty of the civilized world. This was and is the basis of *Hindutva*. The strength of the morality behind this concept cannot be questioned and I challenge the detractors (which includes professors and so-called academics) of *Hindutva* to counter this with rational argument if they have any.

The Supreme Court of India's verdict in 1995 re-emphasized what the proponents of *Hindutva* have been saying all along: it is not a negative philosophy; it is not directed at others. Here is the conclusion of the court.

> It is a fallacy and an error of law to proceed on the assumption that any reference to *Hindutva* or Hinduism in a speech makes

it automatically a speech based on Hindu religion as opposed to other religions or that the use of the word *Hindutva* or Hinduism per se depicts an attitude hostile to all persons practising any religion other than the Hindu religion ... and it may well be that these words are used in a speech to emphasize the way of life of the Indian people and the Indian cultural ethos. There is no such presumption permissible in law contrary to several Constitution Bench decisions.[5]

Hinduism and Hindutva

Hindutva is not synonymous with Hinduism. *Hindutva* is the protective armor of Hinduism. *Hindutva* is an assertive ideology that seeks to protect the practitioners of Hinduism from predatory forces. It is an ideology that seeks to address the grievances of the Hindu community. *Hindutva* aims to shape the society in the image of Sri Ram (one of the most revered Hindu deities, who embodies the concept of the perfect man): strong and powerful, yet humane and compassionate.

Though it may seem paradoxical at times, it is an ideology that seeks to ensure that the secular tenets of Hinduism remain the guiding force of India and is not replaced by some suffocating, intolerant theocracy. One must realize that it was the open nature of Hindu philosophy that made modern India a secular country constitutionally in 1947.

Being a Hindu does not automatically make you a proponent of *Hindutva*, although logically one should be. Millions of Hindus through a combination of subtle misguidance and lack of information are not active promoters of this thought and are even detractors of this ideology. And one need not be a Hindu to be a proponent of *Hindutva*. Any educated person (not just those who have university degrees but people who are knowledgeable about events that have impacted Hindus) with some intellectual capacity for discriminating between right and wrong regardless of his or her religious persuasion will instantly grasp the veracity of this ideology. Such is the case with people like Francois F. Gautier and David Frawley. These are individuals who were not born Hindu, but who by objective, unbiased reasoning have come to the conclusion that Hindus have been wronged and continue to be wronged in present times. It is why these people advocate *Hindutva*.

Do Hindus Require Protection?

As I write this it is July 3, 2004. The Amarnath *yatra* (pilgrimage) is under way in India. But it is shrouded in controversy. The state government of Kashmir, a part of the democratic, secular nation of India, has imposed restrictions on the duration of the *yatra*. They have a point: the *yatra* is a prime target for Islamic militants operating freely within the borders of the so-called secular democratic nation of India. But is it not the duty of the government to provide security and freedom to its citizens to practice his or her religion anywhere in India? Or is that a right exclusive to the non-Hindu and non-Vedic religions? Has one ever heard of any Muslim religious pilgrimage in India being targeted violently by Hindus? When Hindus need protection to practice their religion and curbs are forced on their religious practices, all in a country with an 80 percent Hindu majority, is it wrong to infer that the Hindus, despite being a numerical majority, are a people whose rights need to be safeguarded?

And when a Muslim mob brazenly burns a train-load of Hindus in Godhra (Gujarat) and the reaction of leading political parties is one of tacit approval, what am I to conclude? What followed in Gujarat in 2002 was ghastly and cannot be justified. But note the difference in the reactions. There was universal condemnation of the killings during the riots. Even Modi who has come under heavy fire for his handling of the events never said that it was right.

The Godhra incident, however, evoked a diametrically opposite reaction. According to a great many people, including the national spokesman of the Indian National Congress, it was okay to kill the people on the train because they were Hindu activists; in their own words, they had it coming to them. So what does one deduce from these two contrasting attitudes: when Muslims are killed, it is wrong? But it is okay to kill Hindus if they actively profess their religion? All this, in a democratic secular country called India.

Dynamic Philosophy

Hindutva is not a rigid ideology based on rock-hard commandments propounded by any one individual. Its beginning cannot be traced to any definite point in time or any specific writing. It is a philosophy that evolved over the years reshaping itself with each event that adversely impacted the Hindu and India, and kept changing with the times. It continues to evolve.

Take the example of *Akhand Bharat* (Greater India). *Akhand Bharat* (inclusive of Pakistan, Afghanisthan and Bangladesh) was a concept that was at the core of *Hindutva* ideology in the past and in effect negated the very existence of Pakistan. This notion was based on the premise that the traditional land of the Hindus, extending from Afghanistan in the west to Bangladesh in the east had been lost by a combination of forced conversions and violent invasions and needed to be regained. This is an idea that no longer holds water in the changing annals of *Hindutva* as evidenced by what Advani (leader of the BJP) said on a visit to Pakistan in June 2005: "The emergence of India and Pakistan as two separate, sovereign and independent states is an unalterable reality of history." He indicated that he was stating his party's position to clear "some misconceptions and propaganda about what the BJP thinks of Pakistan."

Advani's statements in Pakistan evoked much controversy. But the issue that raised the most furor was Advani's projection of Jinnah as a secular individual, not of *Akhand Bharat*, testifying to the changing times.

Bereft of sound logic to counter the arguments of *Hindutva*, critics have resorted to digging up past 'dirt' that is not relevant to the present dialogue. Exploding isolated minutiae to accord them undue attention is typical of this genre of writers. One such issue is the 'advocacy of racial purity' by Golwalkar* in a book titled *We or Our Nationhood Defined* published in 1939 (65 years ago). This was brought to my attention by an article in an Indian newspaper the *Telegraph* in April

---

*   Iconic leader of the RSS, 1940–73.

2004.[6] I do not know whether this book is in print or not; by the author's own admission the copy that she came across was "tattered, heavily underlined" and had a torn cover. Despite being an ardent proponent of *Hindutva*, I have not read that book nor found it necessary to do so. I do not deny what he wrote. But it is irrelevant to me. I am interested in *Hindutva* as it relates to current events and not the past, like most of its present-day votaries. It is not necessary to believe verbatim (and we do not) with every teaching of Veer Savarkar or Guru Golwalkar. But neither do we have to negate every other dictum of these nationalists because of one *faux pas*. Moreover, Golwalkar appears to have outgrown this notion that he had harbored in his earlier years.[7]

The movement today is quite different from what it was 50 years ago. It has undergone change. I do not want to be held responsible for opinions expressed or actions that occurred even before I was born. Similarly, I revolt with indignation when somebody accuses me indirectly of Mahatma Gandhi's assassination by virtue of being a *Hindutva* supporter. I admire and respect Mahatma Gandhi. I read his *My Experiments with Truth* when I was in the eighth grade and remain greatly influenced by it. But I also believe in the *Hindutva* movement. I do not find this contradictory at all.

Every ideology has different hues, some more radical than the others. Take, for example, the Communist movement in India. At one end of the spectrum are the Naxalites, who even today indulge in violent protest that involves the killing of innocent people and who do not believe in the democratic process. Do we hold the major Communist parties responsible for the misdeeds of these groups? So why is it that the BJP and the RSS are specifically blamed for every act of individual extremism and the vandalism of fringe elements?

The *Hindutva* movement comprises a wide spectrum. At the periphery are people who hold extreme views, and detractors have made every attempt to promote these extremists as representative of this philosophy. Such attempts are not only fraudulent, but inaccurate, for these extremists do not represent the core values and do not reflect the majority view.

Amartya Sen, the Nobel Laureate (no fan of *Hindutva*) concedes this point in *The Argumentative Indian* (p. 53).

> ... while the hard core of *"Hindutva"* advocates is relatively small, around them cluster a very much larger group, whom I will call "proto-*Hindutva*" enthusiasts. They are typically less zealous than the *Hindutva* champions and are opposed to violence in general (and are typically put off by it)....[8]

He also grudgingly acknowledges that the arguments in favor of *Hindutva* "... are undoubtedly weighty considerations and deserve serious attention and scrutiny."[8]

When viewed in totality, without bias or prejudice, *Hindutva* is certainly not the monster some have made it out to be.

It is certainly not the fascist, supremacist philosophy people would like us to believe it is. *It is a dynamic, progressive modern ideology with a distinct Hindu identity that will ensure India's secular and democratic framework.*

While *Hindutva* may at times appear to be an aggressive doctrine, it continues to be tempered by the guiding principles of Hinduism, namely: *Ekam Sat Viprah Bahudha Vadanti* (Truth is One, Sages call it by Many Names), and *Vasudhaiva Kutumbakam* (The Whole Universe is one Family). It is this philosophy which allowed the people of Hindusthan (land of the Hindus) to shelter the Jews who faced Roman persecution, the Zoroastrians who fled the Islamic sword, and the Tibetan Buddhists fleeing from Communism.

Amartya Sen erroneously concludes in *The Argumentative Indian* (p. 72) that *Hindutva* is a "sustained effort to miniaturize the broad idea of a large India—proud of its heterodox past and its pluralist present—and to replace by the stamp of a small India, bundled around a drastically downsized version of Hinduism." The reality is quite the opposite.

The future of India as a genuine democratic pluralist society is inextricably linked with the fate of *Hindutva*. If *Hindutva* prevails, Hindus will continue to remain in majority in India and so will the principles enshrined in their way of life, namely genuine secularism and acceptance of all religions. And with this the foundations of a secular, democratic republic of India.

Who are the Nazis?

(Detractors of Hindutva have attempted to denigrate this ideology by comparing it to Nazism. This article indicates the flawed nature of such an argument and was written in response to an article in the Daily Pioneer*).*

The article, "Decline of Hindu nationalists will bolster UPA" (*Agenda,* January 1, 2006) tries to pass itself off as a studied political analysis, but in reality is nothing more than a hate rant. The accusations against the BJP are short on facts, bereft of reason, and reek of prejudgment. The author flippantly bandies Nazi terminology without an iota of proof to substantiate his wild charges. An objective analysis of the events in post-Independence India indicates that there are other groups or sections of Indian society that deserve the Nazi label rather than the BJP or Sangh Parivar.

Deliberate misinformation, pogroms, and ethnic cleansing formed the modus operandi of Nazism. Let us see how they have been replicated in India. In an act of disinformation that would put even the notorious Goebbels to shame, the so-called secular groups in India are responsible for committing a monumental fraud on a whole generation of Indians. For nearly 50 years after Independence we were taught about the Aryan invasion theory, a hypothesis not backed by scientific proof, historical evidence and, one that did not conform to even plain common sense. In addition, the widespread killing of thousands of Hindus and the senseless destruction of hundreds of Hindu temples that marked the Muslim invasion of India was intentionally underplayed by Marxist historians. Was this all not indoctrination?

The anti-Sikh carnage of 1984 was a pogrom in the truest sense of the word, by every criterion that goes to define this genre of sectarian violence. It was undoubtedly a one-sided, organized massacre of a specific community instigated, orchestrated, and sustained by the establishment. That it was manufactured is obvious for until then anti-Sikh riots were unknown in Indian history. The Nanavati Commission confirmed the involvement of prominent leaders of the Congress in the pogrom.

On February 27, 2002, 59 Hindus, including women and children, were callously roasted to death within the Sabarmati Express, in a scene reminiscent of Hitler's gas chambers. Anyone who has watched the movie *Schindler's List* will understand. When this horrific massacre failed to evoke an appropriate response from the political community, the pent-up Hindu anger exploded into uncontrollable rage that consumed Gujarat and resulted in the loss of hundreds of innocent lives; that is not something anyone would justify or approve, but also not something one would term a premeditated pogrom.

On the aspect of ethnic cleansing, there can be no better example than the plight of the Kashmiri Pandits. The Global IDP project of the Norwegian Refugee Council is an international non-governmental body working for the welfare of internally displaced people. At the beginning of the century there were close to one million Kashmiri Pandits. Today, not more than 9,000 remain in the Valley according to Global IDP. Others put the figure even lower, at 3,000. Their records indicate that close to 350,000 Kashmiri Pandits, constituting more than 90 percent of the Hindu population of Kashmir, have fled the Valley since 1991 as a result of Islamic militancy. When the population of a specific community is decimated by fear from over one million to less than 10,000 and now constitutes a bare 0.1 percent of the population, there is only one word to describe it: ethnic cleansing. Who is responsible?

Based on the above facts and events, an educated reader can reach a sensible conclusion as to who should carry the Nazi label in democratic India.

2

Naipaul's India: "The Hindu Land is a Wounded Civilization"

In response to his winning the Nobel Prize in 2001, Naipaul averred: "I am utterly delighted, this is an unexpected accolade. It is a great tribute to both England, my home, and to India, home of my ancestors." While England provided him with a place and a language to express his thoughts, the ethos of his writings is clearly his Indian ancestry. Never before has a writer's work been so consumed by the complexities of his origin, compounded by the geographical displacement of his forefathers.

His writings about India, scathingly deprecatory at times, have never gone down well with the Indian intelligentsia. His post-Nobel Prize remark that he had contributed to India's intellectual development was greeted with skepticism and antipathy in India. Nevertheless, a close reading of his works reveals that his three books about India (*An Area of Darkness*,[1] *A Wounded Civilization*,[2] and *India—A Million Mutinies Now*[3]) are, in essence, an accurate, objective picture of the changing scenario in post-Independence India.

Naipaul, the son of Indian immigrants to Trinidad, first visited India in the 1960s. He carries in his mind a carefully cultivated image of India—the land of Gandhi and Nehru, of a great civilization. His shock at the land of his ancestors finds vent in a stinging tirade in *An*

Area of Darkness, ostensibly to mask the deep hurt he himself experiences. Jeffery Paine, author of *Father India*,[4] rightly concludes (p. 157): "*Area* ... is the narrative of a young man not finding the India he expected and not liking the India he finds." India does not live up to his dreams and the young Naipaul lacks the maturity to gauge the strength of an ancient civilization.

Naipaul's disgust at what he sees is exemplified in sentences like: "Indians defecate everywhere. They defecate mostly besides the railway tracks. But they also defecate on the beaches; they defecate on the hills; they defecate on the river banks; they defecate on the streets; they never look for cover" (*An Area of Darkness*, p. 70).

However, his observations are not all gloom and doom. He appreciates the Indian attitude and, deep down in his mind exists a glimmer of hope for the country of his forefathers: "Nowhere are people so heightened, rounded, and individualistic; nowhere did they offer themselves so fully and with such assurance. To know Indians was to take delight in people; every encounter was an adventure. I did not want India to sink; the mere thought was painful" (*An Area of Darkness*, p. 263).

But does his book depict genuinely the India of the 1960s? The answer is yes. Naipaul could not have come to India at a more inappropriate time. It was a country in flux. The initial euphoria of Independence had evaporated, the India–China war of 1962 had deflated its confidence and crushed its philosophy of non-violence, the economy was in a shambles and at the helm was an aging, crestfallen prime minister: certainly not an optimistic picture. So when Naipaul suggests, much to the dislike of some Indians, that there was little intellectual life in India 40 years ago, he is probably right. The guiding principles of India at that time had failed. *Ahimsa* (the Gandhian principle of non-violence) had fallen flat in the face of Chinese aggression, socialism had failed miserably, and the image of India as a beggar with a bowl was gaining currency. Resistant and oblivious to the changing world, India's aging political and intellectual leaders, proponents of this decaying ideology, clung stubbornly to it ruthlessly suppressing any alternative thought process and allowing India to sink deeper and deeper into a quagmire. In the absence of a rejuvenating force, there indeed existed an intellectual vacuum. Though rather harsh, Naipaul rightly concludes: "India has been a shock for me, because, you know, you think of India as a very old and civilized land. One took this idea of an antique civilization for granted and thought it contained the seed of growth in this century.... *India has nothing to contribute to the world, is contributing nothing.*" [italics mine]

On a personal note, he ends: "It was a journey that ought not to have been made; it had broken my life in two" (*Area of Darkness*, p. 289). But return he did; again and again until he had made peace with the civilization of his origin.

Ten years later (*A Wounded Civilization*, 1976) the shock, disgust and anger persist, but in an attempt to assuage his own wounds he conducts a root-cause analysis of India's plight. He concludes that the Hindu land is a "wounded civilization," injured by the British Raj and the preceding Islamic invasion. Again, his strong emotional links with India come to the fore: "India is for me a difficult country. It isn't my home and cannot be my home; and yet I cannot reject it or be indifferent to it; I cannot travel only for the sights. I am at once too close and too far" (*A Wounded Civization*, Foreword, p. x).

Towards the end of the first millennium, India had become an inward-looking society which arrogantly ignored the outside world and this attitude had brought with it its inherent weaknesses and prepared the ground for its impending invasions.

> No civilization was so little equipped to cope with the outside world; no country was so easily raided and plundered, and learned so little from its disasters. Five hundred years after the Arab conquest of Sind, Moslem rule was established in Delhi as the rule of the foreigners, people apart; and foreign rule—Moslem for the first five hundred years, British for the last 150—ended in Delhi only in 1947 (*A Wounded Civilization*, p. ix).

The catastrophic effect that these repeated invasions had on the Hindu psyche are well delineated by Naipaul. Commenting on the decline of the Vijayanagar kingdom, one of the last bastions of Hindu rule during the Islamic invasion, he astutely observes: "I wondered whether intellectually, for a thousand years India hadn't always retreated before its conquerors and whether in its periods of apparent revival, India hadn't only been making itself archaic again, *intellectually smaller*, always vulnerable" (p. 8).

This idea is repeatedly emphasized (p. 43):

> Hinduism hasn't been good enough for the millions. It has exposed us to a thousand years of defeat and stagnation. Its philosophy of withdrawal has diminished men intellectually and not equipped them to respond to challenge; it has stifled growth. So that again and again in India, history has repeated itself: vulnerability, defeat and withdrawal.

And for a thousand years (A.D. 1000–1947) foreign rule suppressed the native intellect and stymied growth of the native civilization. Free of the shackles of alien subjugation, one would have expected to see a positive assertion of ones identity in the post-1947 period. Tragically, this was not to be. India's intellectual power fell into the hands of a myopic Indian intellectual community (largely comprised of Marxist-oriented historians, sophisticated Pol Pots who desired to erase any reference to India's past) who failed to give a sense of direction to free India.

These armchair intellectuals propounded newfangled philosophies that only accelerated its sense of purposelessness. One such concept was secularism. This 'secularism' did not subscribe to the dictionary meaning of the word but took on a totally different connotation in India, a corruption. It led to showering on the non-Hindu communities a set of privileges that could not be justified morally, economically, or legally. More importantly, it expected the Hindu to negate his own identity. Any attempt by the Hindu, however innocent, to assert his identity was dubbed reactionary and divisive. This proved disastrous in terms of India's self-confidence. Naipaul was probably the first person to make this observation and express it in no uncertain terms: "The loss of the past meant the loss of that civilisation, the loss of a fundamental idea of India, and the loss therefore to a nationalist-minded man, of a motive for action. It was a part of the feeling of purposelessness of which many Indians spoke" (*A Wounded Civilization*, p. 61).

Even an attempt to accurately define India's historical past was frowned upon. Over the centuries India had shrunk physically. Its boundaries had receded from the mountains of the Hindu Kush in the west to the deserts of Rajasthan, forsaking in the process even its traditional cradle of civilization, the Indus Valley. Academics foolishly contended that the very fact that India existed now was enough to infer that the Islamic invasion was not detrimental to India. They went on to add that invasions had enriched India. Even if India had shrunk to a sliver of land near the southern tip of India, these intellectuals would seek satisfaction that India still existed, totally oblivious of its loss and incapable of appreciating the magnitude of damage. India not only suffered an intellectual depletion but also a crass intellectual perversion that failed to identify the true cause of its backwardness and thus hampered progress.

Therefore, Naipaul correctly avers (*A Wounded Civilization*, p. 8): "The crisis of India is not only political or economic. The larger crisis is of a wounded old civilization that has at last become aware of its inadequacies and *is without the intellectual means to move ahead.*" [italics mine] I am not certain whether India had "become aware of its inadequacies," but it certainly lacked the intellectual means of progress during that period.

Finally, when Naipaul returns to India in the 1990s (*India—A Million Mutinies Now*), he is more mature and discerning (p. 517).

> What I hadn't understood in 1962, or had taken too much for granted was the extent to which the country had been remade; and even the extent to which India had been restored to itself, after its own equivalent of the dark ages—after the Muslim invasions and the detailed, repeated vandalizing of the North, the shifting empires, the wars, the 18th-century anarchy.

Naipaul now sees the benefits of independence, a crucial catalyst for human growth: "… the idea of freedom had gone everywhere in India." And he observes Indians discovering their own identity (to some extent fuelled by the growth of the nationalist BJP): "People everywhere have ideas now of who they are and what they owe themselves."

Change is present everywhere (p. 517).

> India was now a country of a million mutinies. A million mutinies,
> supported by twenty kinds of group excess, sectarian excess,
> religious excess, regional excess: the beginnings of self-awareness,
> it would seem the beginnings of an intellectual life, already
> negated by old anarchy and disorder. But there was in India now
> what didn't exist 200 years before: a central will, a central intellect,
> a national idea.... What the mutinies were also helping to define
> was the strength of the general intellectual life, and the wholeness
> and humanism of the values to which all Indians now felt that
> they could appeal. They were a part of the beginning of a new way
> for many millions, part of India's growth, part of its restoration.

In summary, India had changed. India was now something to be
proud of. Naipaul had something to be proud of. He is finally at peace
with India, the very essence of his origin and his existence.

After winning the Nobel Prize, Naipaul arrogantly claimed he
helped effect this change in India. What he overlooks is the fact that
he is merely the chronicler of the change, not its instigator. However,
one may also look at this remark from a different perspective. Does it
reflect a deep empathy for India? Does he badly want to be part of its
success?

3

India as an Entity

Consumed by an irrational hatred and guided by a bigoted philosophy, the pseudo-secularists in India have claimed that India as a country never existed before the unification of the princely states by the
British. Nothing can be further from the truth. An assertion of this
type can only be interpreted as a sign of overwhelming ignorance, or it
could possibly be an act of deliberate, sophisticated, disinformation.

Cultural Entity

The concept of *Bharatvarsha* [the Indian nation] stretches back to ancient
times. Although different parts were under the rule of different kings,
the subcontinent as a whole has always espoused—till recent times—one
culture and one social structure. It was and is a cultural entity whose
expanse surpassed narrow political boundaries and encompassed the
whole subcontinent. External invasion was met with a united front.

The Puranas clearly delineate the limits of the country. The *Vishnu
Purana* (2.3.1) and *Vayu Purana* (45.75) state that the land that is to
the south of the Himalayas and north of the Samundaras (Southern
Ocean) is Bharat (India). The lists of holy places and of holy rivers
contain the names that spread from north to south and east to west.
Pilgrimage covered the places from Kailash Mansarovar in the north to
Kanyakumari in the south, Hingulaj in the west to Parashuram Kunda
in present-day Arunachal Pradesh.

Even Jawaharlal Nehru (considered the fountainhead of Indian
secularism by present-day pseudo-secularists) accepted India's cultural

continuity and was proud of it. In his book *Glimpses of World History* (p. 129) he writes:

> Right from the beginning, culturally India has been one, because she had the same background, the same traditions, the same religions, the same heroes and heroines, the same old tales, the same learned language (Sanskrit), the village panchayats, the same ideology, and polity. To the average Indian the whole of India was a kind of punya-bhumi—a holy land. Sankara's choice of the four corners of India for his maths (the headquarters of his order of sanyasins) shows how he regarded India as a cultural unit. And the great success which met his campaign all over the country in a very short time also shows how intellectual and cultural currents traveled rapidly from one end of the country to another.[1]

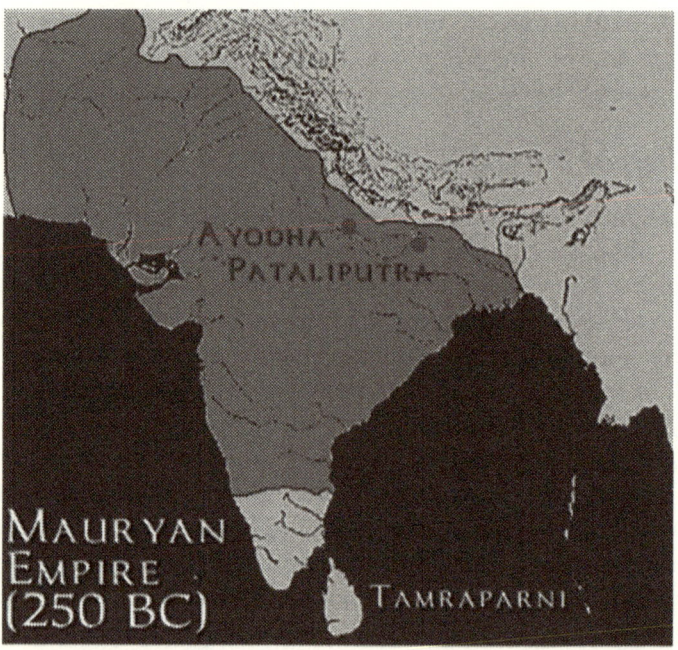

Map 2: India during the Mauryan Empire (250 B.C.)

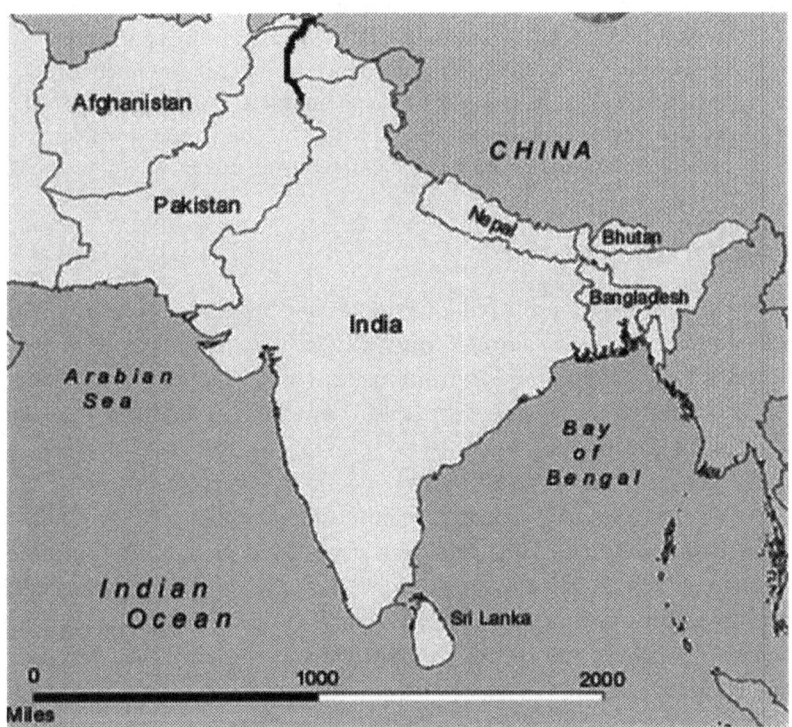

Map 3: Boundaries of Modern India
(not to scale)

Girilal Jain, knowledgeable and esteemed former editor of the *Times of India* avers (*The Hindu Phenomenon: A Unique Phenomenon*, p. 13):

> It is about time we recognize that we are not a nation in the European sense of the term, that is, we are not a fragment of a civilization claiming to be a nation on the basis of accidents of history which is what every major European nation is. We are a people primarily by virtue of the continuity and coherence of our civilization which has survived all shocks. And though inevitably weakened as a result of foreign invasions, conquests and rule for almost a whole millennium, it is once again ready to resume its march.[2]

Political State

Skeptics may dismiss this talk of Puranas and religious places as a fabulous myth, but how can they contradict an objective study of history which clearly supports the continuous existence in some form or other of an Indian state for the last 2,500 years? Few modern states can claim such distinction.

In 269 B.C. (about 2,300 years ago), the Mauryan empire which is to all intents and purposes the forerunner of the modern Indian state both in terms of its territorial expanse as well as its founding principles, extended from Afghanistan in the west to Bengal in the east and from Kashmir in the north to Mysore in the south (Map 2). The remaining part of the Indian subcontinent in the south was ruled by the Pandyas and the Cholas. In an era of constantly-changing boundaries, this empire was able to sustain its vast expanse as a united polity for almost a century; the Mauryan empire lasted till 184 B.C. Even at its zenith (at the end of Aurangzeb's repressive rule), the Mughal empire was barely able to match the boundaries defined by Ashoka; parts of the Indian heartland continued to be under the control of the Marathas and the Rajputs. Moreover, this expansion was too transient (probably a couple of years) to be of any significance, leading historian John Keay to rightly conclude (*India: A History*): "The Mauryan empire was probably the most extensive ever forged by an Indian dynasty; even the Mughals rarely achieved a wider hegemony."[3]

More important than territorial boundaries were the moral principles enunciated during this regime. The spiritual force of the vast Mauryan empire was initially Hinduism, later Buddhism under Asoka. There is no evidence whatsoever of any religious coercion at that time. Ashoka popularized the philosophy of non-violence, tolerance, and equality, which were to become the bases of Indian society for ages to come, till this day. It is befitting that Ashoka's motif of four lions facing the four directions serves as the emblem of modern India.

Compare the map of present-day India (Map 3) with the territorial boundaries of the Mauryan empire: despite alterations at its extremities, the heartland has remained the same. There are few nations in the world that can boast of such territorial continuity over a span of more than 2,000 years. India is not, therefore, a recent creation of the British or any other external force.

In contrast, look at the map of Europe denoting the territorial boundaries in A.D. 1. Not a single modern state that exists today was present at the turn of the last century (Map 4) either in its present physical state or even as an abstract entity. All this only emphasizes the unique identity of India, not as a recent, externally enforced concept but as a distinct age-old entity characterized by the specific attributes of people inhabiting a definite swath of territory.

To credit the British with the unification of India is not only erroneous but ridiculous. This is a manufactured notion that retrospectively found its way into history books of modern India or was implanted there by a set of warped historians. Unity was never a goal or reality of British India. How could it be, when the motto of the British was *divide and rule*? The semblance of unity that one perceived was a chimera that resulted from a series of coercive deals with different rulers that were only meant to serve one purpose: the economic exploitation of India. Moreover, when you turn your attention to the actual lay of the land during that time you realize that there were large areas of India (e.g., Hyderabad, Mysore, etc.) that were beyond British control (Map 5). Hundreds of minuscule kingdoms dotted the landscape at that time. It was the vision and untiring efforts of Sardar Patel (India's first home minister) that was responsible for blending these disparate entities into a modern unified state.

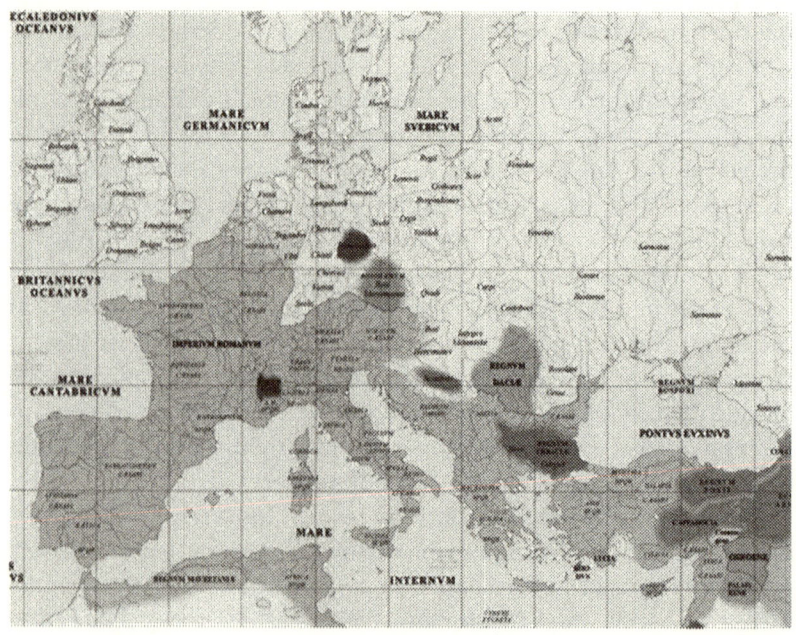

Map 4: Europe in A.D. 1

Map 5: British India

While India continues to exist, a disturbing factor is the shrinking boundaries. As a result of invasion and forced conversions, parts of this entity have seceded and it persists in a contracted state with a definite indication of further diminution.

The Islamic invasion that began in A.D. 700, that is roughly 1,300 years ago, permanently changed the demography of India by an orgy of slaughter and forced conversion. Ever since then, human dignity and freedom have been in peril in the subcontinent. The fact that a democratic secular state exists at all in the central domain of the subcontinent today is because Muslim rule was never able to completely subjugate India or sustain its repressive rule for protracted periods of time without local resistance. The Sikhs, Rajputs and Marathas ensured that Muslim rule never entrenched itself in the heartland of India. Despite the fact that indigenous forces reestablished their supremacy in most areas of the subcontinent, the periods of Islamic rule were sufficient to alter the religious composition of the population by coercion and elimination of non-Muslims. And in those areas where indigenous rule was not reestablished, the outcome was disastrous: parts in the east and west ended up with large Islamic populations and were to become the harbingers of the modern theocratic fundamentalist states of Pakistan and Bangladesh wherein religious tolerance is a rarity.

4

Controversy about History

(During the tenure of the BJP Government [1998–2004], accusations that the BJP was trying to rewrite history abounded. This article takes a critical look at those charges.)

Ever since the BJP assumed power at the federal level in 1998, there have been accusations that the saffron brigade has made a deliberate attempt to distort history and propagate a jaundiced view of past events. Are these charges substantiated by concrete proof? Is there solid evidence of these moves? And the critics, who are now adopting a holier than thou attitude, are their motives and credentials beyond question? Or are these basically vested interests trying to protect their turf? Let us look at both sides of the divide objectively.

The group that is behind this campaign consists of individuals with Marxist leanings who have monopolized the writing of Indian history for the last 50 years. Almost every theory that they have championed has fallen flat in the face of increasing evidence supported by modern scientific techniques. Take, for example, the Aryan–Dravidian theory. British historian John Keay writing in his book, *India: A History* has this to say about the Aryans: "Questions tantamount to heresy amongst an earlier generation of historians are now routinely raised as to who the *arya* were, where they came from, and even whether they were really a distinct people."[1] There is a ton of scientific evidence that has emerged in the past few years that supports this point of view, and effectively demolishes the Aryan–Dravidian concept. A more detailed analysis of this view can be obtained in the following books: *In Search of the Cradle of Civilization*,[2] by Subhash Kak, Georg Feuerstein and David Frawley; and *The Invasion that Never Was*,[3] by Michel Danino.

Another pet theory of these historians involved the destruction of Hindu temples by Muslim invaders. The reasons touted by these seasoned historians as to why Muslim invaders destroyed Hindu temples would make a second-grader blush with embarrassment. Initially, they claimed no Hindu temples were destroyed. Then in the face of irrefutable evidence, they came up with a concoction of reasons as to why these temples were desecrated, the main one being that they were seats of power. But close analysis of historical events clearly exposes the flawed nature of these arguments. More details are available in a series of articles written by Arun Shourie which appeared in the *Indian Express* in the late 1980s, reproduced in *Hindu Temples: What Happened to Them.*[4]

Now who are these people that are opposing the so-called established view? Are they a bunch of retarded, irrational fanatics indulging in juvenile fantasies, or are they scholarly academics who have meticulously studied these matters? Dr Subhash Kak is a professor at Louisana State University; Dr David Frawley is a non-Indian and the director of the American Center of Vedic Studies and author of several books on Indology; Dr N. S. Rajaram is a PhD from Indiana University and the author of several published books; and Arun Shourie is a former editor of the *Indian Express* newspaper. Certainly these people possess eminent credentials and, if one does not agree with their opinions, one should engage in academic debate to challenge the veracity of their stand instead of carrying out a political campaign to suppress their views.

What about the people on the other side of the divide like R. S. Sharma, D. N. Jha, Suraj Bhan, Irfan Habib, Romilla Thapar and Satish Chandra? Are they really objective as they claim? Are their motives and methods above board? Many of them have clearly sided with the Babri Masjid Action Committee, negating an iota of impartiality they may claim to have. Arun Shourie, in *Eminent Historians*,[5] scrutinizes the credentials of these so-called eminent historians and comes up with a picture that is less than complimentary.

Today, these Marxist historians indignantly claim that the saffron brigade is rewriting history, cleverly concealing that they were the ones who actually did it a few years ago. Here are some excerpts from an article by Rajeev Srinivasan that appeared on *Rediff*.[6]

> The West Bengal government in 1989 issued guidelines that said: "Muslim rule should never attract any criticism. Destruction of temples by Muslim rulers and invaders should not be mentioned."
>
> Dated 28 April, 1989, it [the Circular] is issued by the West Bengal Secondary Board. It is in Bengali, and carries the number "Syl/89/1".
>
> "All the West Bengal Government recognized secondary school Headmasters are being informed," it begins, "that in the History textbooks recommended by this Board for Class IX the following amendments to the chapter on the medieval period have been decided after due discussions and review by experts."
>
> Written in Bengali and designated as true (*Shuddo*) and false (*Ashuddo*), some of these deliberate distortions are listed below.
>
> ***Ashuddo:*** "Fourthly, using force to destroy Hindu temples was an expression of aggression. Fifthly, forcibly marrying Hindu women and converting them to Islam was another way to propagate the fundamentalism of the ulema."
>
> ***Shuddo:*** The *shuddo* column reproduces the sentence from "Fourthly" but directs that the entire matter upto "ulema" be deleted from "Fifthly".
>
> ***Ashuddo:*** "Sultan Mahmud used force for widespread murder, loot, destruction and conversion."
>
> ***Shuddo:*** "There was widespread loot and destruction by Mahmud", i.e. no reference to murder or forcible conversion.
>
> ***Ashuddo:*** "Hindu-Muslim relations of the medieval ages constitute a very sensitive issue. The non-believers had to embrace Islam or death".

Shuddo: All matters on this page to be deleted.

Ashuddo: "He looted valuables worth 2 crore dirham from the Somnath temple and used the Shivling as a step leading to the masjid in Ghazni."

Shuddo: Delete "and used the Shivling as a step leading to the masjid in Ghazni."

Is this not rewriting history and a deliberate attempt to deceive the Indian people? Or is such fraud carried out by these 'honorable people' justified?

These are some pressing questions that cry out for answers. For more than 50 years these Marxist historians have had free reign, manipulating history according to their whims and fancies. During this phase, it is surprising that the media did not make an honest effort to scrutinize their conjectures. Additionally, most academics failed to counter or test the veracity of their theories. And the opinions of those who did were effectively suppressed or unceremoniously trashed. The fact that opposing points of view were not given adequate representation in the press and media is something one finds most disturbing, an action that violates the basic tenet of free speech. The intellectual community as a whole must bear some responsibility for the unbridled reign of these Marxist historians. The intellectual community and the press are important guardians of our democracy and must be willing to question people regardless of their position or eminence.

One fails to understand the objections raised by the Marxist historians. For the sake of debate let us momentarily assume that the so-called 'saffron historians' have hijacked the telling of Indian history. Does this in any way prevent the opposition from putting forward their views? Are we living in an authoritarian state? Has anyone gagged their mouths or banned their publications? India is a free country with a free press, radio, and television. They have free access to these media to express their views. Therefore, their protestations appear to have little ground for justification.

Or are they afraid that, shorn of official sanction, their convoluted theories will not stand the test of time? Is it possible that these leftist historians are nervous that their conjectures will not be able to stand the scrutiny of an increasingly aware Indian audience in the face of an opposing point of view? One thinks that these are the true reasons underlying their 'sanctimonious' outrage.

In a communiqué to the Indian History Congress in 2001, President K. R. Narayanan of India said that the politician who looks at history as a quarry from which to dig up grievances for contemporary redress needs to be reminded of the German statesman Otto von Bismarck's remark, "The politician has not to avenge what has happened but to ensure that it does not happen again." If the unsavory aspects of Muslim invasion like temple destruction are suppressed, how will we prevent them from happening again? The callous destruction of the Bamiyan Buddhas clearly indicates that such acts can recur at any time.

To round off his case for a rational and scientific approach to history, the president also quoted a "remarkable judgment" by the Bombay High Court from as far back as 1967:

> It is the right and privilege of every thinker to express his judgment on historical events in a fearless manner. Otherwise, we will not get a true and faithful history of our country. History is not to serve as a hand-maid of a particular school of thought. History must be impartial and objective. To rewrite history according to the views which are popular or which are necessary for bolstering nationalistic egoism or jingoism is a perversion of history.[7]

That is the yardstick that needs to be applied to both sides impartially and not selectively to the saffron brigade if a true and untainted picture of our history is to emerge.

Addendum

On September 12, 2002, the Supreme Court of India upheld the National Curriculum Framework for Secondary Education 2002, rejecting allegations that it was an attempt to saffronize the syllabus for schools.

5

Truth in History: Destruction of Hindu Temples

(During the Muslim invasion and occupation of India that spanned close to a thousand years [A.D. 700–1600], hundreds of Hindu temples were willfully destroyed. In recent times a few historians have sought to justify this malicious destruction with contorted theories. This article exposes the fallacy of their arguments.)

While archeological excavations continue in Ayodhya* to ascertain whether a Hindu temple existed at that site, it is important to revisit how this contentious issue (temple destruction during the Muslim rule) has been presented to our people in the past. Did our historians adhere to the truth? Were they motivated by political considerations? Or did they deliberately attempt to commit a fraud on the Indian people—and the Hindus in particular?

History is the story of the past. It is man's attempt to decipher what happened hundreds or even thousands of years ago. In this endeavor he has had to rely on a varied array of clues like archeological find-

---

* Ayodhya, according to Hindus, was the site of a temple built in honor of Sri Ram, one of Hinduism's foremost deities. Hindus believe that Babur, the first Mughal emperor of India, razed this temple to the ground and erected a mosque in its place which bears his name, Babri Masjid.

ings, notations on rock edicts, and oblique references, mostly indirect evidence. In essence, man has had to put circumstantial evidence together to come to logical conclusions. Despite there being a methodology to this study of the past, history has never been and never will be a precise subject like mathematics or physics. It is to a great extent dependent on human interpretation of findings. And human conclusions are apt to be influenced by a host of factors ranging from ethnic background to one's political beliefs. Therefore, for anybody to claim that his or her interpretation of events is the gospel truth is shortsighted and narrow-minded. But this is precisely what a certain group of historians has done in post-Independence India.

Indian history for the last 50 years or so has been the preserve of historians who were Marxists by conviction and who had come to occupy positions of influence in India's elite universities. They callously distorted past events and interpreted history to suit their political agenda. Their efforts were not an honest attempt at history writing, but a warped exercise in social engineering. Nowhere is this as evident as in the case of the temple desecrations that occurred during the Muslim invasion of India. Opponents (even when evidence was forthcoming) were dubbed fundamentalists and their views effectively suppressed.

A preface to an article, "Temple Desecration in Pre-Modern India" in *Frontline* (December 9, 2000)[1] is a clear example of the vicious propaganda carried out against anybody trying to ascertain the truth or proposing a differing point of view.

> The ideologues of the Hindu Right have, through a manipulation of pre-modern history and a tendentious use of source material and historical data, built up a dangerously plausible picture of fanaticism, vandalism and villainy on the part of the Indo-Muslim conquerors and rulers. Part of the ideological and political argument of the Hindu Right is the assertion that for about five centuries from the thirteenth, Indo-Muslim states were driven by a "theology of iconoclasm"—not to mention fanaticism, lust for plunder, and uncompromising hatred of Hindu religion and places of worship. In this illuminating and nuanced essay on temple desecration and Indo-Muslim states, which *Frontline* offers its readers in two parts, the historian Richard M. Eaton

presents important new insights and meticulously substantiated conclusions on what happened or is likely to have happened in pre-modern India.

Ironically, the use of the words "likely to have happened" in the preceding sentence exposes the frailty of the argument despite the arrogant righteousness of the tone.

During the Muslim invasion of India which spanned over a thousand years, hundreds, even thousands of Hindu temples were destroyed. The vast number of temples destroyed as well as the malevolence with which their desecration took place is ample testimony to the satanic nature of its perpetrators. The following excerpts illustrate the crudity of these actions.

John Keay, a British historian, in his book *India: A History*, had this to say about Mahmud of Ghazni's destruction of the Somnath Temple.

> But what rankled even more than the loot and the appalling death toll was the satisfaction that Mahmud took in destroying the great gilded lingam. After stripping it of its gold, he personally laid into it with his sword. The bits were then sent back to Ghazni and incorporated into the steps of its new Jami Masjid, there to be humiliatingly trampled and perpetually defiled by the feet of the Muslim faithful.

Khushwant Singh in his book, *We Indians* (p. 13), avers:

> Mahmud of Ghazni was only the first of a long line of Muslim idol-breakers. His example was followed by Mongols, Turks and Persians. They killed and destroyed in the name of Islam. Not a single Buddhist, Jain or Hindu temple in northern India escaped their iconoclastic zeal. Some temples were converted to mosques; idols and figurines had their noses, breasts or limbs lopped off; paintings were charred beyond recognition.[2]

What is even more perverse is the fact that these notorious acts were proudly extolled by Persian poets (including the great Persian poet Firdaushi), who defined Mahmud as a paragon of Islamic virtue and a model for other sultans to emulate.

The actual number of temples destroyed during this dark period is contentious. Hindu nationalists claim that over 60,000 temples were destroyed. Leftist historians (and their supporters), while disputing this figure, are now willing to concede that there is proof that at least 80 temples were destroyed (Richard Eaton, "Temple Desecration in Pre-Modern India," *Frontline*, December 9, 2000). *So we now happen to agree upon the fact that at least 80 temples were destroyed by Muslim invaders.* What was once considered to be a fantasy of Hindu chauvinists is now accepted as a reality.

A meticulous look at even this truncated list of desecrated temples is extremely revealing. There was hardly a prominent Hindu temple that was spared and hardly a Muslim ruler who did not indulge in it. This list includes temples from all parts of India, including the south. Further, each and every important Hindu temple appears to have been targeted. Somnath, Mathura, Benares [now Varanasi], Madurai, Kalihasti, Puri, Pandarpur are but a few that appear on this list. Buddhist monasteries at Odantapuri, Vikramasila, and Nalanda in Bihar were also vandalized.

Initially, some historians claimed that such destructions never occurred. But in the face of irrefutable evidence, they conjured up a medley of reasons as to why these destructions were justified. The ridiculousness of these arguments makes them incomprehensible to a sane mind. Let us evaluate each reason rationally.

Premise: *Muslim rulers destroyed temples only during the initial invasion of a kingdom, not when temples were under their jurisdiction.*

This is one of the theories put forward to explain Mahmud of Ghazni's dastardly deeds. Richard Eaton states in *Frontline*: "… the Ghaznavid sultan never undertook the responsibility of actually governing any part of the subcontinent whose temples he wantonly plundered," as though this was justification enough for his crimes. The desecration of a temple, whether during an invasion or not is still desecration and does not in any way diminish the magnitude of the crime. However, for the sake of debate and in all fairness I am willing to test this theory, despite its obvious absurdity. The examples given below (reproduced verbatim)[1] clearly belie the validity of this concept.

a)   In 1478, when a Bahmani garrison in eastern Andhra mutinied, murdered its governor, and entrusted the fort to Bhimraj Oriyya, who until that point had been a loyal Bahmani client, the sultan personally marched to the site and, after a six-month siege, stormed the fort, destroyed its temple, and built a mosque on the site.

b)   In 1659, Shivaji Bhonsle, the son of a loyal Hindu officer serving the Muslim Adil Shahi sultans of Bijapur, seized a government port on the northern Konkan coast and disrupted the flow of external trade to and from the capital. Responding to what it considered an act of treason, the government deputed a high-ranking officer, Afzal Khan, to punish the Maratha rebel. Before marching to confront Shivaji himself, however, the Bijapur general first proceeded to Tuljapur and desecrated a temple dedicated to the goddess Bhavani, to which Shivaji and his family had been praying.

c)   In 1613 while at Pushkar, near Ajmer, Jahangir (a Mughal emperor) ordered the desecration of an image of Varaha that had been housed in a temple belonging to an uncle of Rana Amar of Mewar, the emperor's archenemy.

d)   In 1635, Shah Jahan (a Mughal emperor) destroyed the great temple at Orchha, which had been patronized by the father of Raja Jajhar Singh, a high-ranking Mughal officer who was at that time in open rebellion against the emperor.

Other instances prove the same point.

a)   In 1669, the Mughal emperor Aurangzeb ordered the destruction of the great Vishvanath temple in Banaras which was in his domain. The reason: Shivaji's escape from Banaras had been facilitated by Jai Singh, the *great grandson* (not the son or grandson) of Raja Man Singh, who *may* have built the Vishvanath temple. Jai Singh was not the son or grandson but the great grandson of Raja Man Singh, who may (repeat *may*) have built the temple and, this was enough reason to destroy it. Is this logic? Can a sane man accept this?

b)   In 1670, Aurangzeb supervised the destruction of Mathura's Keshava Deva temple and replaced it with an idgah. The reason: the leader of a local rebellion had been found near the city (not near the temple). Can this be a reason?

c)   In the seventeenth century, Aurangzeb ordered an attack on the Bamiyan Buddhas in Afghanistan. To quote Rakhaldas Sengupta, the former head of an Indo-Afghan team for the restoration of the Bamiyan Buddhas, "Parts of the wooden frame were burned and there was damage to the upper part of the face and the lower lip and hands."

All the above demolitions took place in the respective kingdoms of the Muslim rulers, effectively negating the hypothesis that Muslim rulers did not destroy temples in their domain.

Having failed to find ample proof for this convoluted theory, some historians went a step further. A sub-hypothesis was proposed.

Premise: *Muslim rulers destroyed temples in their domain only to discipline errant subordinates (as though it were justification enough), or to put down a rebellion in those areas.*

Even this far-fetched explanation cannot pass muster. Did they punish disloyal Muslim officers in the same fashion? The answer is a resounding *No*. Infractions short of rebellion normally resulted in demotions in rank, while serious crimes like treason were generally punished by execution, regardless of the perpetrator's religious affiliation. No evidence, however, suggests that ruling authorities attacked public monuments like mosques or Sufi shrines that had been patronized by disloyal or rebellious officers. Nor were such monuments desecrated when one Indo-Muslim kingdom conquered another and annexed its territories. *This further proves beyond any doubt that Hindus and Hindu temples were specifically selected for victimization.*

In contrast, there is not a single instance where an invading Hindu king destroyed or desecrated a mosque or meted out the same treatment to a mosque under his control.

Richard Eaton says in his article, "Temple Desecration in Pre-Modern India" in *Frontline* (December 9, 2000):

> ... when Hindu rulers established their authority over the territories of defeated Muslim rulers, they did not as a rule desecrate mosques or shrines, as, for example, when Shivaji established a Maratha kingdom on the ashes of Bijapur's former dominions in Maharashtra, or when Vijayanagar (a Hindu kingdom in the south of India) annexed the former territories of the Bahamanis or their successors. In fact, the rajas of Vijayanagar, as is well known, built their own mosques, evidently to accommodate the sizable number of Muslims employed in their armed forces.

To recapitulate this bizarre train of reasoning: first, these historians claim that no Hindu temples were destroyed. When this is disproved, they theorize that temples were demolished only by invading Muslim kings and no further destruction occurred when these temples came under their jurisdiction. When even that does not pass muster, they go on to suggest that, when destruction *did* occur in their kingdoms, it was to punish disloyal subordinates. However, even that rational finds no grounds for justification.

Let us stop trying to find justifications for this criminal conduct where none exist. No amount of explanation is going to mitigate the gravity of these dastardly acts. Attempts to whitewash these crimes will only exacerbate the situation. When one denies that a crime has been committed, one perpetrates yet another crime against the victim. Let us have the moral courage to accept them for what they are: hate crimes, plain and simple.

What is the express reason for documenting these ghastly deeds? Is it to hold the present-day Muslims for the wrongdoing of their forefathers? *Certainly not.* Is this recapitulation an attempt to wreak vengeance on the Muslims of today? Again the answer is *No.* Then what is the purpose of this exercise? *As a civilized society, we are duty-bound to ensure that such barbaric acts do not occur in our country again.* The best way to effect this is to remind people continually of such ghastly misdeeds. If we do not do this, we will be doing a great disservice to our future generations.

Further, it is puzzling and disturbing that present-day Muslims consider themselves duty-bound to vindicate the crimes perpetrated by their ancestors. All over the world reconciliation and expression of remorse are the order of the day. President Clinton apologized to the Blacks for slavery, the Australian government expressed regret to the Aborigines, and the Swiss apologized to the Jews they did not save during the Holocaust. The people who asked for forgiveness, in each of these cases, were not the ones who had committed the crime. These magnanimous gestures were meant to soothe past wounds and dispel the rancor in aggrieved hearts. In contrast, the Muslims of the India of today are bent on a path of confrontation, aided and abetted by pseudo-secularists who see this as an opportunity for political gain. Is it so hard to give up Ayodhya, especially when it means so much to the Hindus? This is a question every right-thinking Muslim must ask himself or herself.

To those who say that these events belonged to a time gone by and will not occur again, they only have to remember what happened in Afghanistan recently. The Islamic Taliban ordered the destruction of all idols (Buddhist and Hindu) which reflected Afghanistan's rich history. Included among the list of structures destroyed were two statues of a standing Buddha (in Bamiyan) measuring 175 and 200 feet, among the tallest in the world. Can these destructions be justified as instruments of political conquest?

Simon Wiesenthal, the legendary Nazi hunter, once said, "I see what I am doing as a warning to the murderers of tomorrow. A warning that they will never rest in peace." And that alone is the reason for recalling our unfortunate past: nothing more, nothing less.

6

Changing Demography of South Asia

Demography is defined as the study of population. The demography of a region has a direct bearing on the political structure of a country. When changes in the character or composition of a population occur, it is bound to impact on the social and cultural milieu of the region: this in turn is going to influence the political environment. This is especially so in the subcontinent where religion plays a crucial role in the configuration of the government.

Ideally, religion and state must be kept apart, this being the basis of the modern secular state. But try as we may, religion, willy nilly, influences the political set-up. People who form a part of the state have their personal ideologies or beliefs and these are bound to impact positively or negatively upon the type of government they choose to establish and run.

Most religions are basically undemocratic, each claiming exclusive divine sanction. Invoking this right, most religions have indulged in atrocities against people of other faiths and their institutions. Islamic invaders have been especially notorious in this regard (detailed in other chapters of this book). The vicious religious rampages of the Spanish conquistadores in South America, the inquisitions in Europe in the medieval ages and more close to home in Goa are instances of Christian intolerance. However, in more recent times, Christian nations have successfully separated religion and state and evolved a more sophisticated type of governance as exemplified by present-day secular democracies of the West. The only religion to have a stellar record of tolerance and acceptance of other views is Hinduism. Hinduism and democracy are synonymous. And democracy is synonymous with human freedom and dignity.

Let us look at how the changing demography of South Asia has diminished the Hindu sphere of influence. When I speak of the Hindu sphere of influence, it may appear to have the connotation of a supremacist or expansionist view. But that is not what I intend to convey. Wherever and whenever Hindu influence in South Asia receded, it was replaced with an intolerant and oppressive society. Therefore, for a free society to thrive in South Asia, it is essential that Hinduism not only survives but flourishes. This is not mere speculation or the assumptions of a parochial chauvinist. This premise is sustained by tangible evidence and corroborated by the outcome of a spontaneous scientific trial being played out in front of us in the subcontinent.

Let me clarify this. In medical research there is a research model called a cross-over trial. To test the validity of a hypothesis, in such a model, the environment is held constant while two variables are interchanged to ascertain the outcome. Events in the subcontinent mimic a cross-over trial. The two variables in this case are Islam and Hinduism and the environment is the Indian subcontinent.

In 1947, united India was divided into India and Pakistan. In India, which has a Hindu majority and a Muslim minority, secularism has prevailed with human and religious rights being preserved even under the rule of the so-called Hindu parties. The Muslim population has not only flourished but even surpassed the majority community in terms of growth rate (Table 1). Muslims have their own educational institutions, their own organizations, and even their own personal law. Added to this is a free press that safeguards their civil liberties, although at times one may feel that the press goes overboard in this matter and deliberately violates the rights of the majority community.

Now take the example of Pakistan, another part of the same subcontinent (the environment being constant) where the two variables are interchanged. Here we have a Muslim majority and a Hindu minority. The result: an Islamic state. Religious rights for all intents and purposes do not exist in Pakistan and the population of the

Hindu minority is decreasing both by forced conversions and restrictions. The suppression is total: the voice of the Hindu community is practically unheard of. So complete is this repression that one does not even know that a Hindu population exists in Pakistan. There is no discussion in Pakistani newspapers about Hindus and their rights and no debate in parliament. In effect, they are irrelevant to the state of Pakistan. And our freedom-loving newspapers in India which wax eloquent on free speech and human rights have no time for the human rights of these Hindus; they are dispensable. Forsaken by the mother country (India, to which they belonged) and suppressed by the new state, their emasculation is total; their extinction a dead certainty.

To sum up, one cannot but conclude: *Hindu majority = Democracy + Secularism* and *Muslim majority = Islamic State + Extinction of Minorities*. Take your pick.

Table 1: Growth Rate by Religion

	Unadjusted				*Adjusted**			
	1971	1981	1991	2001	1971	1981	1991	2001
All	24.8	21.4	26.0	22.7	24.8	24.8	23.8	21.5
Hindus	23.7	21.3	25.1	**20.3**	23.4	24.2	22.9	**20.0**
Muslims	30.8	22.9	34.5	**36.0**	31.2	30.8	32.9	**29.3**
Christians	32.6	13.7	21.5	**22.6**	36.0	19.2	17.0	**22.1**
Sikhs	32.3	26.0	24.3	18.2	32.0	26.2	25.5	16.9

* Excludes Jammu & Kashmir and Assam for all decades from 1961 to 2001.

The Census 2001 population figures for India and Manipur exclude those of Mao maram, Paomata and Purul subdivisions of Senapati district of Manipur.

No Census conducted in Assam in 1981 and in Jammu & Kashmir in 1991.

(*Source:* Census of India, *Census of India Online*, http://www.censusindia. net)

Table 2: Hindu and Muslim populations in India, Pakistan and Bangladesh

Country	Hindu	Muslim	Total
India*	827 (80.5%)	138 (13.4%)	1,027
Pakistan**	2 (1.6%)	126 (96%)	132
Bangladesh***	12 (10%)	115 (90%)	127
Total	**841**	**379 (29%)**	**1,286**

(figures rounded off to the nearest million)
*   2001 India Census figures
**   1998 Pakistan Census
***   2001

Table 3: Percentage of Hindus in Pakistan and Bangladesh at present compared to 1947

Country	1947	Present
Bangladesh	29	10
Pakistan	23	1.6

Table 4: Percentage of Muslims in India at present compared to 1947

1947	Present
10	13.4

Now let us take a look at some hard statistics. In 1947, the Hindu population of Pakistan comprised 23 percent of the total population. Today it makes up barely 2 percent. What happened to the rest? So is the case with Bangladesh. According to normal projections, Bangladesh was expected to have 32.5 million Hindus in 1991.[1] However, census data indicated a population of only 12.5 million. Where did the missing

20 million go? Forced conversion, forced marriages, and forced migration. A look at Fig. 1 and Table 3 clearly indicates that the extinction of Hindu minorities in Pakistan and Bangladesh is imminent.

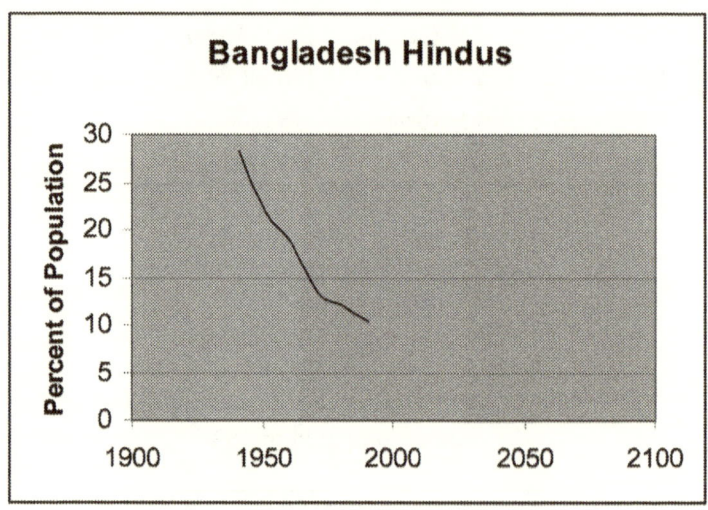

Fig. 1: Hindu Population (Bangladesh)

Compare this with the graph for Muslims in India (Fig. 2). Need I say more? *Hindutva* is not an alarmist response to a nonexistent threat. The threat is *real*, and this is evident when one makes an objective study of the changing composition of the Indian population.

Changing Population

While the changes in Pakistan and Bangladesh have been effected directly, the demographic alteration in India is occurring in a more subtle manner by:

1) Increased growth rates; and

2) Uncontrolled immigration from Bangladesh.

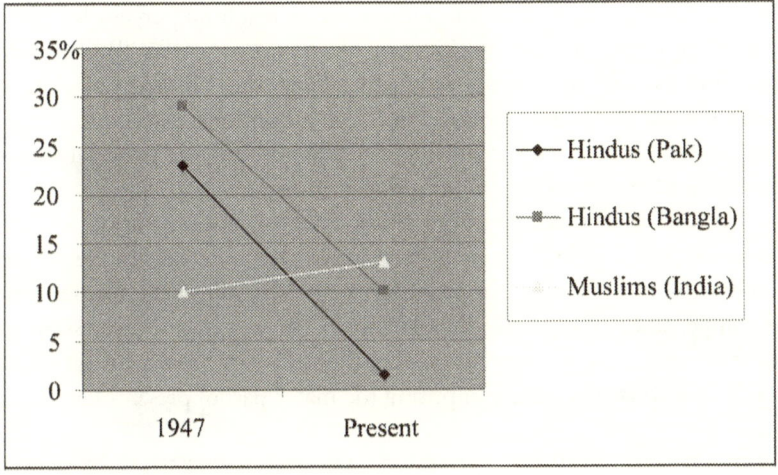

Fig. 2: Increasing Muslim population (in percent) in India in contrast to the decreasing Hindu population of Pakistan and Bangladesh

Growth Rate

Overall across the country, the Muslim population is increasing at a disproportionate rate compared to the rest of the population (Table 1). Muslims in India accounted for 10.7 percent of the population in 1961, 11.2 percent in 1971, 11.4 percent in 1981, and about 12.1 percent in 1991.[2] In 2004, the Muslim population accounted for 13.4 percent (Table 4).

Thirteen percent may not seem an intimidating number and the majority mark of 51 percent may seem a distant possibility. But a country is no corporate board where you need a 51 percent stake to have your way. One must bear in mind that Pakistan was created with less than 30 percent majority of pre-Partition India. So every percentage rise has a distinct impact. And with a total national population in excess of 15 percent you can expect to see distinct changes in the type of governance, social norms, and cultural values. The increasing role of Shariat in resolving Muslim affairs in direct contradiction of Indian law in recent times is a clear pointer in that direction.

According to conservative population projections using the present growth rate (and excluding the increase by uncontrolled immigration), one would expect the Muslim population to reach 20 percent by 2051 and close to 30 percent by the turn of the century (Fig. 3). Towards the later part of the twenty-second century, the Muslim population will overtake the Hindu population. The consequences of these demographic alterations will be profound affecting both the political structure as well as the territorial boundaries of India.

I predict that (unless there are drastic changes) the present democratic secular republic of India in its present format has a maximum lifespan of another 50 to 100 years. The boundaries of India will shrink further with the appearance of a greater Bangladesh in the east and the secession of Kashmir in the north. The twenty-second century will see the emergence of a full-fledged Islamic state comprising the major part of present-day India.

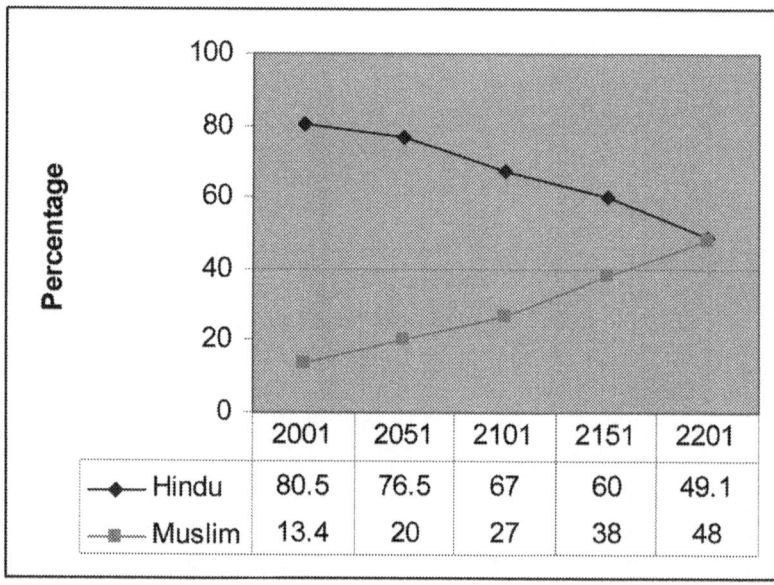

	2001	2051	2101	2151	2201
—◆— Hindu	80.5	76.5	67	60	49.1
┄┄▦┄┄ Muslim	13.4	20	27	38	48

Fig. 3: Population Estimates (by religion) over the next two centuries

* Figures are approximate and based on the present growth rate derived from the 2001 Census and are presented to depict a trend. Results calculated using Human population calculator: http://www.metamorphosisalpha.com

Uncontrolled Immigration

While the present-day 13.4 percent applies to the nation as a whole, there are pockets in vulnerable areas that already have a Muslim majority and can pose serious strategic problems for the security of the country as a whole. The present population of Muslims is calculated to be 31 percent in Assam and 25 percent in West Bengal and is concentrated in an arc of land that adjoins Bangladesh. This arc also involves a part of Bihar which similarly has a high Muslim population.

Arun Shourie presents a lucid analysis of this issue in "Right on Course" (*Indian Express*, October 9, 2004) wherein he clearly depicts the danger of a third nascent or full-fledged Islamic state emerging in India's northeast. In support of his contention he draws extensively from a report filed by T. V. Rajeswar (former governor of West Bengal). Most of the data which follow and the accompanying tables are drawn from that article.

First, let us examine those districts in West Bengal (Tables 5, 6) that border Bangladesh. Perusal of the tables indicates that the Muslim population in these areas is increasing rapidly and stands at dangerous levels. Growth rates registered by the Muslims in these bordering districts clearly outstrip those of the non-Muslim population with rates ranging from 18.5 to 34.2 percent (vis-à-vis 0.7–22.7 percent of non-Muslims). The percentage of Muslims in all these border districts is in excess of 20 with rates as high as 64 percent (Murshidabad), 50 percent (Malda), and 38 percent (South and North Dinajpur).

Table 5: Percentage growth of population during 1991–2001 in districts of West Bengal

District	Muslim	Non-Muslim	Total
South 24 Parganas	34.2	11.5	20.8
North 24 Parganas	23.0	22.6	22.7
Nadia	21.9	18.8	19.5
Murshidabad	28.4	16.4	23.8

District	Muslim	Non-Muslim	Total
Malda	30.7	19.4	24.7
Kolkata	19.0	0.7	3.9
South and North Dinajpur	31.9	22.7	26.1
Jalpaiguri	31.3	20.4	21.5
Cooch Behar	18.5	12.8	14.2

Table 6: Muslims as a percentage during the same period

District	1991	2001
South 24 Parganas	29.9	33.2
North 24 Parganas	24.2	24.2
Nadia	24.9	25.4
Murshidabad	61.4	63.7
Malda	47.5	49.7
Kolkata	17.7	20.3
South and North Dinajpur	36.8	38.4
Jalpaiguri	10.0	10.8
Cooch Behar	23.4	24.2
Total West Bengal	**23.6**	**25.2**

As you follow this belt north into Assam (Tables 7, 8), the situation is even more frightening. Dhubri has a Muslim population of 74 percent, with Goalpara, Hailakhandi and Karimganj all boasting a Muslim population of greater than 50 percent. In all these districts the Muslim growth rate surpasses the non-Muslim growth rate.

Table 7: Percentage growth of population during 1991–2001
in districts of Assam adjoining Bangladesh

District	Muslim	Non-Muslim	Total
Dhubri	29.5	7.1	22.9
Goalpara	31.7	14.4	23.0
Hallakandi	27.2	13.3	20.9
Karimganj	29.4	14.5	21.9
Cachar	24.6	16.0	18.9

Table 8: Muslims as a percentage of population in districts of
Assam bordering Bangladesh

District	1991	2001
Dhubri	70.4	74.3
Goalpara	50.2	53.6
Hallakandi	54.8	57.6
Karimganj	49.2	52.3
Cachar	34.5	36.1

Moving west across West Bengal into Bihar, this zone includes
Kishanganj district with a 68 percent Muslim population. Adjacent
districts of Purnea, Araria and Katihar have Muslim populations ranging from 37–42 percent. In these three districts the growth rate of
Muslims is at least 10 percentage points higher than the rest of the
population.

Even way back in 1991, with less impressive numbers the scenario
was disturbing. Out of a population of 28 million in the border districts of West Bengal, Muslims accounted for 17 million, leading T. V.
Rajeswar to sound a warning: "There is a distinct danger of another

Muslim country, speaking predominantly Bengali, emerging in the eastern part of India in the future, at a time when India might find itself weakened politically and militarily." And judging from the trend, this is a distinct possibility, in Arun Shourie's words, "... the creation of a third Islamic State out of India is 'right on course'." My own prediction is that these areas will be co-opted into a Greater Bangladesh.

It would be naive to assume that these demographic changes are involuntary and purely the consequence of an economic imbalance resulting in migration of poverty-stricken masses to areas of greater economic opportunity. This is a calculated strategy that seeks a greater living space or lebensraum for the Bangladeshi, endorsed by Bangladeshi intellectuals and covertly supported by the government through deliberate inaction.

Below are excerpts from an article written by prominent columnist Sadeek Khan in the Bangladeshi newspaper *Holiday* (October 18, 1991) and referred to by Governor Lt. Gen. S. K. Sinha in his report[3] on illegal immigration into Assam.

> The question of lebensraum or living space for the people of Bangladesh has not yet been raised as a moot issue. All projections, however, clearly indicate that by the next decade, that is to say by the first decade of the 21st century, Bangladesh will face a serious crisis of lebensraum. No possible performance of population planning, actual or hypothetical significantly alters that prediction.
>
> It is said that a borderless world has become the prime requisite for economic growth under the new world order. In fairness, if consumer benefit is considered to be better served by borderless competitive trade of commodities, why not borderless competitive trade of labour? There is no reason why Bangladesh should not insist on a globalized manpower market as consumer markets of nation-states are being progressively globalized under the dictates of monetarists. There is no reason why regional and international cooperation could not be worked out to plan and execute population movements and settlements to avoid critical demographic pressures in pockets of high concentration. There is no reason why under-populated regions in the developed world

cannot make room for planned colonies to relieve build-up of demographic disasters in countries like Bangladesh.

We shall hope for the best in international cooperation. We shall hope for the best in accommodation from the developed world. In reality, nevertheless, Bangladesh may expect little external relief in the short run on the issue of lebensraum. It is also doubtful that Bangladesh may develop sufficient sustainable urbanization or can engineer sufficient reclamation of habitable land from its offshore potential to settle its projected population growth in the next decade. A natural overflow of population pressure is therefore very much on the cards and will not be restrainable by barbed wire or border patrol measures. The natural trend of population overflow from Bangladesh is towards the sparsely populated lands of the South East in the Arakan side and of the North East in the Seven Sisters side of the Indian subcontinent.

So what we see here is an ostensibly rational plea to accommodate the increasing Bangladeshi population, but also a *fait accompli* that Bangladesh will not attempt to prevent; in other words, India's northeast is fair game for the land-strapped Bangladeshis.

Lurking beneath this economic facade is also a sinister religious design that is being actively orchestrated and assisted by our political rulers who pander to vote banks, clearly oblivious of the grave security risk that this poses to India.

An examination of the adjoining areas of Bangladesh is very revealing, especially the districts of Rajshahi, Naogaon, Natore, Joypurhat, Rangpur and Bogra. In these regions of Bangladesh, there is a burgeoning Taliban-type Islamic movement aided and abetted by Al Qaeda and Saudi money.[4] Central to this movement is the radical Islamic group Jagrata Muslim Janata Bangladesh led by Bangla Bhai, which claims a membership of over 100,000. Bangla Bhai himself is a veteran of the jihad in Afghanistan and an avowed follower of Osama bin Laden. Public hangings and kidnappings are routine in this area and serve to enforce a strict Islamic code of conduct. Hindus, Christians and Buddhists live in perpetual fear. A dangerous mix of fear and monetary inducement continue to fuel this apparition which is clearly influencing the adjacent areas on the Indian side. That these areas are being targeted is no coincidence. This is a diabolical ploy aimed at eroding the boundaries of a non-Islamic state and thereby weakening its basic structure. Will the Indian government and the so-called secular press wake up to this real threat? Or will it continue to expend its energy pursuing the nonexistent bogey of Hindu fundamentalism?

Part Two

Kashmir

Kashmir is at the core of Indian nationhood.

—Jaswant Singh, Minister for External Affairs
(1998–2002)

7

The Kashmir Dispute: A Different Perspective

Kashmir has been a bone of contention between India and Pakistan for the last 60 years. However, in the last decade, fuelled by Pakistan's nefarious activities, this dispute has become more intense and terrorism has turned this land, once described by the Mughal emperor Jahangir as a paradise on earth, into a veritable hell.

According to the present political set-up the players in this dispute include the Indian government, Pakistan, the Hurriyat,* and the separatist groups that represent mainly the Muslim population of Kashmir. Although New Delhi has occasionally met with the Buddhists of Ladakh and representatives of the Hindu minority, the focus has been with dealing with the militants and other groups that cater mainly to the Muslim constituency of Kashmir. Is the role of these players justified? Do they have a moral right to be there? Does history support their contention? Or have they thrust themselves into the issue by sheer thuggery?

So let us look at this issue from a moral, ethical, and historical standpoint devoid of its present political contortions.

The first question is: Who really owns Kashmir? The Muslims, the Hindus or the Buddhists? For the sake of debate let us entertain the premise that it is the Muslims who possess this right because of their

---

*   Conglomerate of separatist Kashmiri groups.

numerical superiority. Can this be justified? Brute majority cannot be the basis of such a claim especially in a democratic civilized society. It is against the pluralistic values of our traditions. As Jaswant Singh, India's foreign minister during the NDA government (1998–2004), succinctly put it: "India does not believe in a denominational definition of nationalism. The state of Jammu and Kashmir is at the core of the nationhood of India." In addition, can you imagine the disastrous consequences this inference can have on the Muslims and Christians in Hindu-majority states?

At times, the Hurriyat has suggested that this is not about religion but about *Kashmiriyat.* But is this really so? In the last decade nearly a quarter million Kashmiri Hindus have been driven out of their homes in an ethnic cleansing that surpasses Bosnia. On the eve of Clinton's visit to India in March 2000, militants killed 34 Sikhs in cold blood in Chattisinghpora. Later that year in August more than 20 Hindus on their way to the holy shrine of Amarnath were massacred by terrorists. While the Hurriyat may excuse itself by claiming that these dastardly acts are the handiwork of non-Kashmiris, it cannot pass muster. Have they made any specific attempt to stop this victimization of minorities? Their condemnation of these acts has been muted. Also, one finds it difficult to believe that this direct targeting of the Hindu minority is being done without the tacit moral, material, and logistic support of the majority. The Muslim majority of Kashmir has to bear the blame, at least to some extent, for the ethnic cleansing of the Kashmiri Hindus. As an accessory to this horrendous crime, they lose any moral authority on this issue.

Further, the Hurriyat has diabolically misinterpreted almost every terrorist act to wrongfully malign India. Prem Shankar Jha writing in *Outlook* (June 25, 2001, The Bad Faith Factory) had this to say about the Hurriyat.

> When Mirwaiz Maulvi Farooq was killed on May 21, 1990, everyone blamed Governor Jagmohan and India, when the killing had been carried out by two members of the Pakistan-based

---

*   Kinship of all Kashmiris regardless of religion.

Hizbul Mujahideen. When H. N. Wanchoo, Kashmir's greatest human rights activist, was killed in December 1992, the blame was pinned on BSF chief Ashok Patel and Governor Saxena, when the murder had been committed by members of the Jamiat-ul-Mujahideen, a front organization created by the ISI.* The Chattisinghpora massacre was similarly blamed on the security forces despite the initial statements of the widows that foreign militants were responsible.

This confusion isn't accidental but carefully manufactured by various militant groups, above all the Hurriyat. One or more members of its executive council have been in the vanguard of every accusation against India, while in the name of unity the others, who have known better, have remained silent. When the Sikhs of Chattisinghpora were massacred, Hurriyat chairman Abdul Ghani Bhat carefully refrained from ascribing blame and asked for an international inquiry. He knew perfectly well that India would never agree and that this would strengthen the suspicion that it was responsible.

Therefore, despite its sanctimonious claim to being the true representative of the Kashmiris, the fact that they have never stood up for the Kashmiri Hindu and the fact that they have willfully played along with the terrorist agenda deprives the Hurriyat of any moral or legal right to represent Kashmir or Kashmiris.

What is the basis for Pakistan's claim to Kashmir? In 1947 when India was partitioned into India and Pakistan, the princely states were given the option to choose either Pakistan or India or even remain independent. Initially, the Maharaja of Kashmir, Hari Singh, chose to remain independent, but when Pakistan sent hordes of Pathan tribesmen (*razakars*) to forcibly take over Kashmir, Hari Singh hastily changed his mind. He signed the Instrument of Accession and asked for India's help. Sheikh Abdullah, the undoubted leader of the Kashmiri masses, also ratified this agreement. A great deal of confusion surrounds the Instrument of Accession and the conditions detailed in it. Some indicate that it was unconditional; others suggest that the

---

*   Inter-Services Intelligence (Pakistan's spy agency).

right of self-determination was built into it. However, one thing is clear: *there is no mention whatsoever of merger with Pakistan. If that was the case, then where did Pakistan get the idea that it had a claim to Kashmir?*

Further, in 1947 the UN had pronounced Pakistan as the violator of international law when it invaded J&K. Subsequently, the will and wishes of the people of J&K were lawfully enshrined in the state's Constitution of 1957 that irrevocably bound the state to India from that year forever. *Pakistan has thrust itself into the equation, not by dint of moral virtue or legal principle, but by illicit force as epitomized by its shameless support of blatant terrorism.*

What about the Kashmiri Hindus? Do they have a right to this land, despite the fact that only a handful of their kin remain in the Valley? The ethnic cleansing of Hindus in Kashmir is the latest in the long line of atrocities perpetrated by the Muslims on the Hindus of Kashmir. History is replete with the sufferings of Hindus at the hands of their Muslim rulers. The Pathan rule during 1752–1819 was the darkest period in the history of the state. The most notorious of these kings was an Afghan ruler called Sikander. A Muslim historian, Hassan, gives a detailed account of Sikander's atrocities in his book, *History of Kashmir.* The edict at that time was: "Either adopt Islam, or accept death or banishment." Hindus who refused conversion were tormented and Hindu scriptures were either burnt or thrown into the Dal Lake. Not a single village or town was spared. Temples were destroyed by the hundreds, including the famous Martand temple that took almost a year to be demolished. Fear drove many Hindus to convert, migrate, or commit suicide.

Certainly, a historical wrong cannot be rectified by committing another one today. But neither is there a need to confer legitimacy on these dastardly acts. Passage of time cannot mitigate the heinous nature of these deeds. They should be remembered for what they are: hate crimes, pure and simple.

My purpose in recalling these historical events is to pose the question that if a people are decimated by forcible conversion or driven out of the land by sheer terror, do they lose the right to the land? If so, does this not go against the basic tenets of human civilization? Does this not violate the pluralistic tradition of our society?

Dr Vijay K. Sazawal, National President of the Indo-American Kashmir Forum, writing in *Outlook* (June 27, 2001, Framework for Peace in Kashmir) had this to say about the rights of the non-Muslims of Kashmir.

> Just because Pandits, Dogras and Ladakhis have not resorted to violence does not mean that their demands are any less important or urgent. This is one of the most common mistakes made by outside observers who customarily equate violence with severity of demands, not fully comprehending the *totally non-violent* culture that has historically existed in Kashmir among the non-Muslim communities.

Let me also interject two unlikely players into this dispute: Indians as a whole, and the Hindus of the rest of India in particular. Do the Hindus from other parts of India have any claim to this land? Kashmir is not an island. It never was and never will be. It is a part of our culture. A historical review certainly proves it. Old Hindu scriptures clearly detail the origin of Kashmir. According to the oldest extant book on Kashmir, *Nilmat Puran*, in Satisar lived a demon called Jalod Bowa, who tortured and devoured the people. Hearing the suffering of the people, Kashyap, a great saint of our country, came to the rescue of the people there. After performing penance for a long time, he was able to cut the mountain near Varahmulla, which blocked the water of the lake from flowing into the plains below. The lake was drained, the land appeared, and the demon was killed. The saint encouraged people from India to settle in the Valley. The people named the Valley as Kashyap-Mar and Kashyap-Pura from which the word Kashmir is derived.

Mythology apart, the Hindus have certain legitimate rights to this land. Many of their most important holy shrines are located in this land: Vaishno Devi temple and Amarnath to name two. Thousands of Hindus from all over India make a pilgrimage to Amarnath every year despite the danger from Islamic terrorists. So what would be the fate of this pilgrimage in an altered geopolitical situation? Or would the Hindus be asked to sacrifice these holy shrines as they were asked to do so in 1947 when swaths of traditional lands became part of Pakistan?

India is a federal union and every state is to some extent dependent on the others. Kashmir more so than other states has been the beneficiary of the taxpayer's money. No Indian state has the right to unilaterally secede from the union after deriving benefits for 60 years.

In conclusion, Kashmir is woven into our tradition. Kashmir has been a part of Bharat for ages. It has always been a part of India and that is where it belongs: an integral part of a democratic, pluralistic society providing shelter and equality for all humans, Hindu, Muslim, Sikh, and Buddhist. It cannot be a part of a religious state that discriminates against other faiths. In 1947, we betrayed over 5 million Hindus and Sikhs (left behind in Pakistan) and sacrificed them to the tyranny of a theocratic state. This cannot and should not be repeated.

8

Kashmiri Pandits:
Ethnic Cleansing the World
does Not See

Pogroms and ethnic cleansing represent the ultimate evil in the litany of hate crimes. Sadly, free India has experienced both. The anti-Sikh carnage of 1984 was a pogrom in the truest sense of the word by every criterion that goes to define this example of sectarian violence. It was undoubtedly a one-sided organized massacre of a specific community instigated and orchestrated by the establishment.[1] The greater tragedy was the fact that we as a nation deliberately and callously failed to acknowledge for more than 20 years the political machinations that galvanized and transformed a public emotion into a satanic exercise of murder, arson, and loot. The publication of the Nanavati Report in 2005 and the subsequent resignation of a cabinet minister, though belated, did assuage hurt wounds and reaffirm to some extent the rule of law. More important, it tells me that we remain a civilized nation; we still possess the ability to discern right from wrong. We have not become numb to these humane concepts.

While I am comforted by this thought, another event directly challenges this premise and questions our ethical fidelity, our commitment to principles, and our ability to defend the values enshrined in our Constitution. When a quarter million people belonging to a specific community are driven from their homes to become refugees in their own country, when thousands of families see their abodes go up in flames right before their eyes, when men have to endure the agony of their daughters and wives being blatantly molested in their presence or carted away as booty and we, as a people and a nation choose to remain mute spectators, what does it say of us? Yes, this is the heart-rending tale of the Kashmiri Pandits, forsaken and forgotten by a society of which they are a part, ignored by a press that is supposed to champion the cause of the oppressed, and betrayed by a nation of which they are citizens. This is the ethnic cleansing the world—and more importantly India—chooses not to see and appears to have forgotten.

To drive home the magnitude of the crime that is occurring, let me cite some statistical data. These are figures derived from independent international organizations. The Global IDP project of the Norwegian Refugee Council is an international non-governmental body working for the welfare of internally displaced people. Their records indicate that close to 350,000 (three and a half lakh*) Kashmiri Pandits have been displaced from the Valley, constituting more than 90 percent of the Hindu population of Kashmir.[2] The exodus has not stopped; unopposed threats by militants ensure its continuity. In 2004, another 160 of the remaining 700 families fled the Valley.

Kashmiri Pandits are the original inhabitants of Kashmir with a culture and tradition that goes back 5,000 years. At the beginning of the century there were close to 1 million Kashmiri Pandits. Today, not more than 9,000 Pandits remain in the Valley according to Global IDP. Others put the figure even lower, at 3,000. Data from the National Human Rights Commission indicate that Kashmiri Hindus made up 15 percent of the population in 1941. By 1991, their numbers had dwindled to comprise a mere 0.1 percent of the population. These are the stark facts that tell the tale of the Kashmiri Hindu. When the population of a specific community is decimated by fear from over 1 million to less than 10,000 and now constitutes a bare 0.1 percent of the population, there is only one word to describe it: ethnic cleansing. No amount of explanations, no amount papering over can contradict

---

*   One lakh is equal to 100,000.

this harsh reality. Neither can this be wished away as the propaganda of Hindu communalists. Figures don't lie. In addition at least 1,000 Pandits have been killed and close to 16,000 homes have been burnt. To sum it all up: 350,000 displaced; over 1,000 killed; and at least 16,000 homes burnt. Let these figures sink in for you to decide for yourself the enormity of this human calamity.

The world has seen other instances of attempted ethnic cleansing in modern times, but that of the Kashmiri Pandits stands out as the only one that has been carried out to completion with near-total eradication of a community from a region. While in Rwanda and Bosnia the numbers involved were larger, the redeeming feature was that the international community stepped in, aborted the ethnic cleansing and reversed the situation. In contrast, nothing of that sort is in the offing in Kashmir, making it by far the largest and worst case of successful ethnic cleansing.

While the Kashmiri Hindu has been at the receiving end for a couple of hundred years, the present saga of ethnic cleansing can be traced back to January 1990. To make one understand what they underwent and what they had to endure, I am going to *graphically recreate* those events. Picture a Kashmiri Pandit living in a small town in a lush valley surrounded by tall mountains, just like his ancestors have done for hundreds of years. Then suddenly the serenity of his existence is disrupted by the unfolding events of 1990. On January 4, 1990, *Aftab*, a local Urdu newspaper in Srinagar, runs a press release issued by the Hizbul Mujahideen, proclaiming jihad and asking all Hindus to leave the Valley. Both friends and foes exhort him to go; foes threatening dire consequences and friends fearful for his safety.

Initially, he resists, but the tension keeps mounting. Doors are dotted red and walls are plastered with posters and handbills, asking all Pandits to leave. Masked men with Kalashnikovs roam the streets forcing people to reset their watches and clocks to Pakistan Standard Time.

And then one fateful day, the pressure reaches its zenith. As dusk approaches, his family members cower inside their home, behind the false security of their doors, while outside the exhortations become louder and shriller. The muezzin's routine call for prayer to the Islamic faithful is replaced by three taped slogans that resonate throughout the cold January night, its eerie darkness accentuating the fear instilled by these repeated incantations:[3]

"Kashmir mei agar rehna hai, Allah-O-Akbar kehna hai" ("If you want to stay in Kashmir, you have to say Allah-O-Akbar"): Is this consistent with our philosophy of secularism?

"Yahan kya chalega, Nizam-e-Mustafa" ("What do we want here? Rule of Shariat"): does this conform to the Constitution of India?

"Asi gachchi Pakistan, Batao roas, te Batanev san" ("We want Pakistan along with Hindu women, but without their men").

Can you imagine the depravity of this thought? It violates every basic tenet of human nature. Can any society, any people allow such an edict to be proclaimed publicly and still call themselves civilized? Can you imagine the plight of that family huddled together in fear and desperation as this degenerate rant rasps against their eardrums? Is this land a part of Hitler's Germany, Aurangzeb's Mughal kingdom, or a part of democratic, secular, civilized India, you wonder.

In this setting, the local state government abdicates its responsibility, the federal government feigns ignorance and the rest of India doesn't even bat an eyelid. Thus began the exodus which continues uninterrupted to this day, to cease only when the last Pandit has left the Valley.

While it is easy to blame Islamic militants and point a finger across the border, it cannot absolve us of our responsibilities. There was a total failure, at every level of the defense mechanisms that define a civilized nation and a civilized world: society, government, press, human rights commissions and Amnesty International—all abrogated their responsibility.

Society has a duty toward each of its members, especially its minorities. While it cannot be asked to shower unnecessary privileges on its minorities, it is duty-bound to protect them especially in times of danger. When a society exudes a strong moral fabric, no external force can specifically target a section of its population. What happened in Kashmir could not have occurred without the tacit compliance of the majority Muslim community and so, despite their protestations, they must share a significant proportion of the blame for this atrocity.

Look at other parts of India: pockets of minorities live their lives unhindered among overwhelmingly Hindu populations. Yes, transient instances have occurred as in Gujarat, but society stepped in, the press carried out a relentless campaign, NGOs (Non-Government Organizations) took the crusade to even distant lands and resolved the problem. The victims were not left to fend for themselves: therein lies the difference.

When society fails to protect its weak, the government is duty-bound to intervene. But how effective has been the role of the Indian government? While the deployment of troops to curb militant activities is commendable, it has not created a secure environment for the return of the Kashmiri Pandits. Further, the reluctance of the government to adopt an unequivocal stand vis-à-vis the return of the Pandits has only emboldened the militants. In one instance, when the Hurriyat made a half-hearted attempted to facilitate the return of the Pandits, the militants opposed it vociferously and promptly killed 5 Hindu shepherds in Rajouri to drive home their point. And what did the Indian government do? It maintained a stoic silence.

The government's attitude towards the Kashmiri Pandits is baffling, to say the least. Internally Displaced Persons (IDP) are entitled to international humanitarian aid and, more important, protection by international organizations. Wary of putting Kashmir on the international stage, it has refrained from labeling the Pandits as IDPs, but at the same time is loath to adopt stringent measures to enforce its diktat.

Fear of offending the sensibilities of the Muslim majority has even prevented the government from including the Pandits in the negotiating process. Their relatively small numbers and non-violent approach (which should increase their stature) has only added to their marginalization despite India's claim that they do not subscribe to a denominational concept of statehood.

Amnesty International projects itself as the standard bearer of human rights across the world. Its preamble states:

> AI's vision is of a world in which every person enjoys all of the
> human rights enshrined in the Universal Declaration of Human

Rights and other international human rights standards. In pursuit of this vision, AI's mission is to undertake research and action focused on preventing and ending grave abuses of the rights to physical and mental integrity, freedom of conscience and expression, and freedom from discrimination, within the context of its work to promote all human rights. AI is independent of any government, political ideology, economic interest or religion. It does not support or oppose any government or political system, nor does it support or oppose the views of the victims whose rights it seeks to protect. It is concerned solely with the impartial protection of human rights.

However, when its track record with respect to the Kashmiri Pandits is evaluated, its claim appears to be shallow and suspect. Of the nearly 200 notifications pertaining to India released by Amnesty International during the period 2000–5, only one made any significant reference to the Kashmiri Pandits. Perusal of the annual reports of 2000–5 reveal the same disregard for the sufferings of the Kashmiri Pandits; only the 2004 report contains a passing reference to the Nandimarg massacre that took the lives of 24 Pandits, including 11 women and children.[4]

Direct efforts to involve AI have also not been successful. When an exhibition titled "Terrorism Unleashed" highlighting the plight of the Kashmiri Pandits was held at the prestigious Commonwealth Club in London and the organizer sought to invite the local representative of AI, she cried off citing excessive workload: so much for their commitment to human rights.

Now what about the press and the several secular NGOs that pride themselves as being the champions of human rights? Can they claim to have done their duty? The answer is No. The amount of newsprint devoted to this matter falls way short of the amount required to do justice to this burning issue. Similarly, while the NGOs hold passionate conferences in prestigious universities all over the world proclaiming to the world the deficiencies of the Indian system in protecting the rights of the Muslims, none of their seminars have highlighted the plight of the Kashmiri Pandits. Token articles have graced the pages of their limited-subscription magazines lest they be accused of political incorrectness, but sincerity of purpose is lacking. The National Human Rights Commission has not been helpful either.

When we expect such high standards when non-Hindu minorities are involved, why this callous indifference towards the minorities in Kashmir? Why this laxity in the implementation of our secularism? Is it because the minorities are Hindus? I hate to believe that this is the cause for this negligence. Or do the lofty ideals of our republic crumble when faced with a gun-toting aggressive Muslim majority? These are the questions that cry out for answers.

What is even more galling is the cold indifference exhibited by other Indians to the hapless condition of their own brethren. Their indifference is tantamount to a crime and does not augur well for the country as a whole. I leave the reader with this quote from Martin Niemöller (1892–1984) of Germany to mull over.

> In Germany they came first for the Communists and I didn't speak up because I wasn't a Communist. Then they came for the Jews and I didn't speak up because I wasn't a Jew. Then they came for the trade unionists and I didn't speak up because I wasn't a trade unionist. Then they came for the Catholics and I didn't speak up because I was a Protestant. Then they came for me—and by that time no one was left to speak up.

9

Amarnath: A Lesson in Secularism

My aunt is 73 years old. She lives with her family in a small town in Maharashtra* near the Karnataka* border. She is a pious woman who makes a *padyatra* (a pilgrimage on foot) from Pune to Pandarpur every year covering the distance of over 250 kilometres in two weeks. But when she told me a few days ago that she planned to make the trip to Amarnath this year, I panicked. The specter of a terrorist attack flashed through my mind. Hadn't the terrorists just blown up Bridge no. 2 at Chandanwari on the route to the cave temple on May 24? I expressed my apprehension but she replied in a calm, determined voice that she would go to Amarnath and that her God would protect her. But the question in my mind is: Will the Indian state protect her? Has the Indian state done everything it can to protect the right of the Hindu to worship in India vis-à-vis the Amarnath *yatra*? A nonsensical and fantastical query with a hint of Hindu chauvinism at the outset but one which reveals a harsher truth when examined closely.

My other motive in narrating this incident is to emphasize the importance of Kashmir with its innumerous holy Hindu shrines to the common Hindu people of India, like my aunt who lives thousands of miles away. No part of India is an island. Centuries of tradition and culture have woven this land into an interlocking entity with no one

---

*   Indian states.

people or individual being able to claim exclusive ownership of any part of it despite being a numerical majority in that region or area. It belongs to one and all as long as they conform to the pluralistic principles of our nation.

Located at a height of 13,000 ft above sea level and tucked away among the mountains of the Himalayas, Amarnath is a cave temple that houses a naturally formed ice structure that is worshipped by Hindus as a form of Shiva (one of the trinity of Hindu Gods). Amarnath has been a revered holy shrine for Hindus for more than 3,000 years. The first recorded pilgrimage to Amarnath took place in 1000 B.C. and has continued uninterrupted till the early 1990s when terrorists began to target this *yatra*.

In 1994, the Harkat-ul Mujahideen (an Islamic militant group) forbade pilgrims from visiting this shrine. Despite all the talk of *Kashmiriyat* (a regional kinship that supposedly includes both Hindus and Muslims), no Muslim group or the Hurriyat (a loose federation of Muslim groups fighting for self-control of Kashmir) came out strongly against this diktat. However, this threat failed to dissuade the common Hindu from visiting the shrine. In fact, the number of Hindus visiting Amaranth has steadily increased since then. In 2004 a total of 150,000 pilgrims trekked up to this mountain shrine, a testimony to the grit and courage of the common Hindu.

The Islamic terrorists followed up their initial warning with actual acts of violence in subsequent years. Attacks on innocent pilgrims became routine with each episode becoming more ghastly and callous than the preceding one.[1] In 2000, two militants armed with AK-47s emerged from the jungle lining the route and fired indiscriminately, killing 30 unarmed pilgrims and leaving 60 wounded. What was even more despicable than this barbaric act was that the terrorists indulged in a macabre dance of evil joy at the conclusion of their satanic mission. The next year, another terrorist attack left 12 people dead, including 7 pilgrims and 5 workers. And in 2002, in a pre-dawn terrorist attack on the Nunwan camp en route to the shrine, 8 more people were killed and many more injured.

In addition to the environment of fear that challenges the pilgrim, logistic roadblocks, albeit well-intentioned, also abound. A cumbersome registration process has become the rule and inconvenient time restrictions for the duration of the *yatra* have been imposed in the guise of security demands and of all the reasons, pollution concerns. Every year sees a public spat between Governor Lt. Gen. S. K. Sinha, the chairman of the Amarnath Shrine Board and the state government regarding the timing of the *yatra*. The year 2005 was no different, with the state government even approaching the high court to resolve the issue. So what should be a peaceful journey for spiritual solace turns out to be an onerous task fraught with uncertainties and anxiety.

For a moment step back and analyze this scenario objectively. For a moment, forget the fact that these pilgrims are Hindus and this is a Hindu *yatra*. Substitute the word Hindu with the name of any other religion. Wouldn't you conclude that there is a blatant attempt to curb the religious freedom of this people? Yes, there are extraneous factors and these are unusual circumstances. But it is precisely in such adverse situations that the strength of a government and the moral convictions of a people are tested.

Now let us look at who should bear responsibility for this sorry state of affairs. Pointing a finger across the border cannot absolve us of our responsibilities to protect our citizens against the nefarious ventures of alien forces. I am willing to accept that the central government has shown a sincere resolve by deploying increasing number of security personnel despite claims to its ineffectiveness. Even the shenanigans of the state government can be dismissed as arising out of genuine concerns. But what about the role of the local population?

There have been mass demonstrations by the Kashmiri people against the so-called atrocities of Indian security forces. I have no argument with that as protest is an integral part of democracy. But has there been even a single mass demonstration against this wanton killing of unarmed Hindu pilgrims? Has the Hurriyat told its militant partners in no uncertain terms to desist from interfering with the Amarnath *yatra*? Has anyone issued a fatwa against the killing of innocent pilgrims? No. On the other hand the Hurriyat's formal condemnation of these acts has often been combined with distasteful innuendo directed against the Indian government. After the Nunwan massacre, the Hurriyat called for an "impartial investigation" and stated: "Pilgrims have been attacked in the past and though the government had ordered an inquiry once, its report was not made public, nor any action was taken against those found guilty," suggesting that the Indian government had something to hide with regard to these incidents.

Every citizen has a defined role in a society to ensure peace and harmony. This is not the exclusive responsibility of the government establishment alone. Further, the majority community has a responsibility towards the minority community and also vice versa. Has this principle been fulfilled when we look at the issues related to the Amaranth *yatra* and the ethnic cleansing of Kashmiri Pandits? Foreign terrorists cannot succeed in their evil designs without the tacit support of the local population and, therefore, the local Muslim population must bear some responsibility for these sordid acts.

On the lines of this reasoning let us look at the rest of India. The media in India are quick to pillory the VHP, Bajrang Dal and RSS (Hindu nationalist groups) and portray them purely as merchants of religious hate. If this were really so, how difficult do you think it would be in an overwhelmingly Hindu country for these groups to impose informal sanctions on non-Hindus from visiting their holy places in India, similar to what is happening with Amarnath? Easy. Right. But then how come there is not a single instance of a Muslim or Christian being prevented by fear from paying obeisance at his or her holy site of worship? My purpose in making this point is not an arrogant claim to moral superiority, but to try and ensure that events be viewed impartially and objectively, so that the right efforts are made in the right direction. Only then can we have a just and honest society.

10

A Hindu CM for J&K: Any Takers?

(This article was written when the only Muslim-majority state in India, Kashmir, was getting ready to appoint a new chief minister [governor in the United States] in November, 2005 and provides insight into how the political system is loaded against the Hindu. Kashmir is geographically divided into three areas: the predominantly Muslim Valley, Hindu Jammu, and Buddhist Ladakh.)

As the November 2 deadline for the change of guard in Srinagar (capital of Kashmir) approaches, numerous interesting options present themselves: Should Mufti Mohammed Sayeed be left alone to complete a full six-year term in the interest of continuity? Or should he be replaced by a Congress chief minister as per the accord reached three years ago? A long list of Congress aspirants have already made themselves available: the frontrunner, Ghulam Nabi Azad; Rajya Sabha MP* Saifuddin Soz; former PCC** chief Ghulam Rasool Kar; and present PCC president Peerzada Mohammed Sayed. Who from this motley pack should be the "chosen one"? What traits must the incumbent chief minister possess? Should he be from the Valley or hail

---

*   Member of Parliament.
**   Pradesh (state) Congress Committee.

from Jammu? These are the questions uppermost in people's minds. But I wish to pose another: Why not a Hindu chief minister?

Democracy is not synonymous with brute majorityism. Embedded in a civilized democracy are subtle nuances that transcend mere numbers and which exhibit a refined compassionate element that carries with it all sections of a society however minuscule they may be. Every action in a democracy must reflect this true spirit of egalitarianism, not merely subscribe to the letter of the ideology. And this principle is all the more important to bring about unity of purpose in a country like India in which every region boasts of myriad religious, lingual, and cultural diversities that outwardly appear to be at conflict with each other.

Indian democracy has done exceedingly well when measured by this parameter. After the horrendous Gujarat riots, Atal Behari Vajpayee, the prime minister of India (1998–2004) of the BJP (which has often been labeled as anti-Muslim), brought about a consensus to appoint Abdul Kalam (a Muslim) the president of India. This symbolic gesture was meant to alleviate the nervousness of the minority community, instill a degree of confidence and, above all, convey this important message: we care.

Despite the perpetual debate on secularism and communalism, religious bigotry has not been the hallmark of Indian democracy. There has not been widespread outrage or even a murmur of protest when a Muslim has been elected as the chief minister of predominantly Hindu-majority states. Abdul Gafoor was the chief minister of Hindu-majority Bihar which has a Muslim population of only 16.5 percent. Maharashtra, a supposed bastion of *Hindutva* with a mere 10 percent Muslim population had no qualms about accepting Abdul Rehman Antulay as its chief minister. Other Hindu-majority states like Kerala, Assam, and Pondicherry have also had Muslim chief ministers. It is this secular, impartial element that defines Indian democracy and which is the raison d'être for its success.

Let us examine how the state of Jammu and Kashmir shapes up when viewed against this background. Despite being touted as the only Muslim-majority state in a predominantly Hindu India, J&K is not a homogeneous entity, either in its geographic distribution or religious composition. The Kashmir Valley, the most vociferous of its components, comprises barely 16 percent of its landmass compared to Jammu that accounts for 26 percent and Ladakh that makes up 58 percent. Even in terms of human population, the predominance of the Valley is more a matter of hype than a fact-based reality: Jammu has 45 percent, Ladakh 3 percent, and Kashmir 52 percent. Nevertheless, all the chief ministers of J&K since Independence have come from the Valley. In keeping with the tenets of our democracy, it is time that someone else (other than from the Valley) don the premier mantle.

Further, all the chief ministers of J&K have been Muslims as though conforming to an unwritten law. Hindus constitute 33 percent of the combined population of J&K, with Muslims making up 64 percent and the remaining 3 percent being accounted for by Buddhists, Sikhs, and Christians. When Hindu-majority Maharashtra with a Muslim population of 10 percent can have a Muslim chief minister, can anyone have an objection to J&K with a Hindu population of 33 percent having a Hindu chief minister?

Better still if a Kashmiri Pandit can be made the chief minister. Would it not atone for the ethnic cleansing that has gone on? Will it not encourage the Pandits to return? I am sure the usual excuses will be put forward like the intricacy of the Kashmir issue and the exceptional nature of the problem. These I view as merely a facade to further vested interests and thwart adherence to honest principles.

The true validity of an ideology is tested in trying times and the ability to apply the principles of democracy and secularism, impartially and in a just fashion is what distinguishes a civilized society from a barbaric one. Would it not be a shining example of Indian democracy and Indian secularism, if a predominantly Muslim state accepts a Hindu chief minister? Will we fail this test or will we come out with flying colors?

P.S.: This did not happen: Ghulam Nabi Azad, a Muslim, became the chief minister in 2005.

Part Three

Contemporary India

This is the secret of the political history of modern (medieval) India. Weakened by division, it succumbed to invaders; impoverished by invaders, it lost all power of resistance, and took refuge in supernatural consolations; it argued that both mastery and slavery were superficial delusions, and concluded that freedom of the body or the nation was hardly worth defending in so brief a life. The bitter lesson that may be drawn from this tragedy is that eternal vigilance is the price of civilization. A nation must love peace but keep its powder dry.

—Will Durant, *The Story of Civilization*

The crisis of India is not only political or economic. The larger crisis is of a wounded old civilization that has at last become aware of its inadequacies and is without the intellectual means to move ahead.

—V. S. Naipaul, *A Wounded Civilization*

11

Lies, Lies, and More Lies

When I read recent reports (fabricated, to say the least) of the IDRF (India Development Research Fund, a charity organization) being a conduit for the communal violence in Gujarat, I said to myself, "There we go again." There just doesn't seem to be an end to this litany of lies. A few years ago there was a story circulating in the Indian news media about the fleeing Hindu refugees from Kashmir. These reports claimed that over a quarter million Hindus had left their homes in Kashmir, not out of fear of Islamic militancy, but at the instigation of Jagmohan, the then governor of Kashmir. It was and still is a ridiculous notion without an iota of truth, a blatant lie. But it didn't stop some of our intellectuals from propagating that falsehood.

Then did you hear that the 34 innocent Sikhs of Chattisinghpora, who were murdered in cold blood on the eve of President Clinton's visit to India in 2000, were not done in by Islamic militants, but by agents of the Indian government in order to discredit the separatist movement? Another canard spread, not by Pakistan, but by our own so-called intellectuals.

This has been the pattern ever since the BJP came to power in India in March 1998. In fact, there has been a relentless witch-hunt, the likes of which we have never seen before, one orchestrated by major English newspapers in cahoots with the opposing political parties and so-called secular groups, one that knows no logic and sees no reason and one so consumed by a blind hatred for the BJP that fraud and deceit are considered appropriate weapons in this mad orgy; a witch-hunt in which even national interest is of no concern.

Beginning in the late 1990s, Indian newspapers reported on a rash of so-called anti-Christian incidents perpetrated supposedly by Hindu extremists. Close scrutiny, however, revealed that these incidents were deliberate falsehoods spread by vested interests to further their political agenda.

Take, for example, the incident in Jhabua, MP (Madhya Pradesh, a central Indian state) in which four nuns were brutally raped. Even before any details of this crime were available, the major newspapers had conducted a trial, established the criminal guilt of Hindu extremists, and communicated this message to the country and the world at large by splashing this news across their front pages.

It was finally left to Francois Gautier, the correspondent in South Asia for *Le Figaro*, France's largest-circulated newspaper, who went to Jhabua to unearth the truth. This is what he wrote in the *Hindustan Times* (February 1, 1999).[1]

> This massive outcry on the "atrocities against the minorities" raises also doubts about the quality and integrity of Indian journalism. Take for instance the rape of the four nuns in Jhabua. Today the Indian Press (and the foreign correspondents—witness Tony Clifton's piece in the last issue of *Newsweek*) are still reporting that it was a "religious" rape. Yet I went to Jhabua and met the four adorable nuns, who themselves admitted, along with their bishop George Anatil, that it had nothing to do with religion. It was the doing of a gang of Bhil tribals, known to perpetrate this kind of hateful acts on their own women. Yet today, the Indian Press, the Christian hierarchy and the politicians continue to include the Jhabua rape in the list of the atrocities against the Christians.

A few days later, the home minister (secretary for internal security) released a list of the criminals, a list forwarded to him by the Congress (whose leader incidentally happens to be Christian) government of Madhya Pradesh: 12 of the accused were Christians! Christian groups initially questioned this finding, but when confronted with irrefutable proof chose to ignore it. And the newspapers? Yes, they reported it in some hidden corner of their papers. What about those things called truth and honesty? Do they matter? No. According to their warped sense of values, maligning the Hindu groups is synonymous with truth.

About another incident that occurred in Kerala, Francois Gautier wrote:

> In Wyanad in northern Kerala, it was reported that a priest and four women were beaten up and a Bible was stolen by "fanatical" Hindus. An FIR (first information report, a police complaint) was lodged, the communists took out processions all over Kerala to protest against the "atrocities" and the Press went gaga. Yet as an intrepid reporter from the Calicut office of the *Indian Express* found out, nobody was beaten up and the Bible was safe. Too late: the damage was done and it still is being made use of by the enemies of India.

More recently, the reporting of events in the troubled state of Gujarat are other examples of hyperbole. Before elaborating on specific instances of deception, let me state that we cannot and should not condone the senseless violence that happened there. By the same token, we also cannot accept the malicious dissemination of falsehoods.

Writing about the Gujarat riots, noted novelist Arundhati Roy said ("Who's She When She's at Home?" *Outlook*, May 6, 2002):

> A mob surrounded the house of ex-Congress MP Iqbal Ehsan Jaffri. His phone calls to the director-general of police, the police commissioner, the chief secretary, the additional chief secretary (home) were ignored. The mobile police vans around his house did not intervene. The mob broke into the house. They stripped his daughters and burnt them alive. Then they beheaded Jaffri and dismembered him.[2]

The description is graphic, the veracity of the incident taken almost for granted coming from a writer of Arundhati Roy's reputation. But, alas, that's where we make the mistake. Fame and honesty are not interlinked, as the following paragraph clearly indicates.

Jaffri was killed in the riots but his daughters were neither 'stripped' nor 'burnt alive.' T. A. Jafri, his son, in a front-page interview titled

"Nobody Knew My Father's House was the Target" (*Asian Age*, May 2, Delhi), says, "Among my brothers and sisters, I am the only one living in India. And I am the eldest in the family. My sister and brother live in the U.S. I am 40 years old and I have been born and brought up in Ahmedabad."

So if Ehsan Jaffri had only one daughter (singular) who was safe and sound in the United States, where did Roy get her facts about not one but daughters (plural) being stripped and burnt? Was it the fantasy of a writer's mind? Or was it willful deceit aimed at maligning her ideological adversaries?

Arundhati Roy did apologize for her mistake in a letter published in *Outlook*, May 27, 2002.[3] Could this have been a genuine mistake, one is tempted to ask? But when such 'mistakes' occur periodically, the chances of their being accidental appear remote. They appear to be, in fact, calculated machinations aimed at achieving a specific goal, as the following incident further proves.

In the same article, Roy claims:

> Last night a friend from Baroda called. Weeping. It took her fifteen minutes to tell me what the matter was. It wasn't very complicated. Only that Sayeeda, a friend of hers, had been caught by a mob. Only that her stomach had been ripped open and stuffed with burning rags. Only that after she died, someone carved "OM" on her forehead.

Disturbed by the thought of such a ghastly act, Balbir Punj (a BJP member of parliament) had this matter investigated. He wrote in *Outlook* (July 8, 2002):

> Shocked by this despicable "incident," I got in touch with the Gujarat government. The police investigations revealed that no such case, involving someone called Sayeeda, had been reported either in urban or rural Baroda. Subsequently, the police sought Roy's help to identify the victim and seek access to witnesses who could lead them to those guilty of this crime. But the police got no cooperation. Instead, Roy, through her lawyer, replied that the police had no power to issue summons. Why is she hedging behind technical excuses?[4]

So when asked to prove her allegations, Arundhati Roy developed cold feet: definitely not the attitude of a crusader for truth.

Similarly, you may have read some accounts of what preceded Godhra. There were wild accounts of an altercation between Ram *sevaks* (Hindu pilgrim devotees of Lord Ram) and Muslim stall-owners, and of abduction of a Muslim girl by Ram *sevaks*. All this emanated on the basis of a fictitious e-mail, as revealed by Prem Shankar Jha (*Outlook*, March 25).

This also reminds me of an episode that occurred a few years ago. Film maker Pradip Kishen (Arundhati Roy's husband and a part of the same ideological group) walked out in a huff from the National Film Awards jury accusing the board of political motives. He asserted that Raveena Tandon (well-known Indian actress) had been given the best actress award for the film *Daman* because she had campaigned for the BJP. When an angry Raveena asked him to prove his charges, he beat a hasty retreat and submitted an unconditional apology. This may not be an item of national importance, but serves to confirm the fact that certain groups repeatedly use questionable methods to achieve their broader political aims.

Mr Tunku Varadarajan is an editorial features editor of the *Wall Street Journal*. He also has had several publications in the *New York Times*. This is an excerpt from his article "Deadly Zeal in India" (*New York Times*, January 11, 1999).

> This happened a month after a Roman Catholic priest was murdered and religious fanatics vowed to turn an entire district into a "Christian-free zone." In keeping with this promise, a chapel was set on fire. Elsewhere, armed men broke into a Catholic convent and assaulted two nuns inside, and another Catholic priest was shot dead.[5]

This report appeared exactly *15 days before, I repeat 15 days before* Graham Staines, the Australian missionary was killed in Orissa. Until then no Christian missionary had been killed in India as a result of religious hatred, yet Tunku Vardarajan's op-ed piece described picturesquely how armed men broke into a convent and shot dead a Catholic priest. In deference to fair play and before passing judgment,

I e-mailed the newspaper asking them for details that I may not have been aware of. I never received a reply. A week later, however, the *New York Times* reported that no lives had been lost in the so-called anti-Christian campaign. (This was before the Staines murder.) So this was without doubt a calculated lie with an ulterior motive. Apart from being a tall tale it was also a clever ploy: exaggerate the crime, evoke greater condemnation, thereby silence those who do not agree with you. What do these incidents suggest? The so-called secular groups (more appropriately, 'pseudo-secular') are willing to go to any lengths to put across their point of view, even if it involves duplicity, spreading half-truths or indulging in hyperbole. How can we believe a people or the philosophy they espouse when trickery is an indispensable item in their communication? Can an ideology that requires the crutches of deceit and distortion sustain itself?

Even more disturbing, many eminent personalities (Nobel laureates, software entrepreneurs, and academics) are using their prestige to lend misplaced credibility to these untruths. But one must remember that shorn of the sophisticated accents that we speak in, of the Queen's English that we pen, of the academic degrees from Western universities that we flaunt, of our status or fame in society that we impose upon others, what really matters is the truth and honesty of what we write or speak. When judged by this yardstick, some of these so-called intellectuals and eminent personalities fall into an abysmal pit of moral bankruptcy that is hard to fathom. Blind adherence to any ideology whether it be *Hindutva* or anti-*Hindutva* will lead us nowhere. Truth, honesty and justice must surmount all ideology. Double standards and hypocrisy, especially the type practiced by our so-called eminent personalities will only destroy our democracy and society. Truth must be the basis of any ideology. Truth and honesty must be the foundations of our society.

So let us stop lying. Let us be fair—and above all, let us speak the truth. Then alone can we build a truly democratic and secular India.

12

The Babri Masjid Controversy

(Ayodhya, according to Hindus, is the site of an ancient temple built in honor of Sri Ram, one of Hinduism's foremost deities. Hindus believe that Babur, the first Mughal emperor of India, razed this temple to the ground and erected a mosque in its place which bears his name, Babri Masjid. This structure has been a bone of contention between Hindus and Muslims for over 300 years. Hindus wish to build a temple dedicated to Sri Ram at this site. The controversy reached its zenith in December 1992 when this edifice was inadvertently or otherwise torn down by the thousands of Hindu activists who had collected there to express their fervent hope.)

I offer no reasons. I give no excuses. I only ask this question: In return for the thousands of Hindu temples destroyed, all that I am asking for is an unused, disputed, decrepit religious structure that happens to be at a site that I believe is the birthplace of my most revered God. Is that asking for too much?

13

Hindu Anger

(The Hindu-Muslim riots that occurred in Gujarat in March 2002 were covered widely by both the local and international media and portrayed as an example of an evil majorityism. The concept of Hindus in India being a majority is deceiving. A thousand years of repressive Islamic and British rule have transformed a numerical majority into a dysfunctional minority. Hindutva aims at redressing this imbalance without disturbing India's tradition of pluralism. The following article traces the events that led to the gruesome riots.)

It was 7:30 AM on February 27, 2002 as the Sabarmati Express (named after Mahatma Gandhi's legendary ashram) pulled into Godhra, a middle-sized town predominantly Muslim in population in the western Indian state of Gujarat. The train was carrying Hindu Ram *sevaks* (worshippers, pilgrims, or activists) made up of elderly Hindu women sporting *bindis* (large, round decorative spots of color on their foreheads), young children and men returning from Ayodhya, the birthplace of the foremost deity (Sri Ram) among the Hindu pantheon and now a disputed place of worship between Hindus and Muslims. Many Hindus believe that, in the late sixteenth century, Babur, the founder of the Islamic Mughal Empire, tore down a temple that existed at Ayodhya and replaced it with a mosque (not in use). Now Hindus wish to regain the land and rebuild a temple at the same spot; hence the dispute.

On the railway platform, it was business as usual just like what one comes across in the thousands of railway stations across the vast expanse of India: tea vendors selling cups of sweet, milky tea; hawkers parading their array of snacks; and small boys with sheaves of early-morning newspapers moving from compartment to compartment. The train paused at Godhra for three minutes before resuming its journey to Ahmedabad.

What happened next was anything but usual. The train abruptly came to a stop five minutes later. A crowd of over two thousand Muslims materialized suddenly as if out of nowhere. Before the passengers realized what was happening, the doors were systematically bolted from outside, the train doused with cans of petrol and set aflame. Shrieks of burning women and children could be heard above the war cries of the mob outside as the train was converted into a blazing inferno. The emergency services just did not arrive in time, or were prevented from reaching the hapless victims by the mob that chanted gleefully from the sidelines. When the embers cooled a few hours later, 59 charred bodies lay motionless among the rubble.

India had not seen such an exhibition of sectarian violence for nearly 50 years. Whatever the provocation, it did not merit such a barbaric retribution and nothing can mitigate the callous nature of the crime. To the Hindu pilgrims, who hoped to one day build a temple to Ram at Ayodhya, it was déjà vu. More than 10 years earlier, Mulayam Singh Yadav, the then chief minister (governor in the U.S. system) of Uttar Pradesh and who draws his political strength from an anti-Hindu pro-Muslim platform, had ordered his police to mercilessly gun down a similar group of pilgrims: 40 unarmed Hindus died in that episode.

As the news of this macabre incident spread throughout the country, the anger welling up amongst the Hindu believers was almost palpable. Surprisingly, the sense of outrage which should have been universal was selective and muted. The vulgarity of the silence was resounding. There was no instant condemnation from the Muslim community, and when it did come a whole 24 hours later it was too late. On television talk shows across the country, political leaders, including those from the Congress Party, subtly hinted that the Hindus had it coming to them in order to justify this ghastly act, prompting even Vir Sanghvi, the editor of the *Hindustan Times* and a harsh critic of the Hindu resurgence movement to ask (editorial, *Hindustan Times*, February 28, 2002): "Have we become such prisoners of our own rhetoric that even a horrific massacre (of Hindu activists) becomes nothing more than an occasion for Sangh-Parivar (read Hindu)–bashing?"

Nobody tried to reach out to the shocked Hindu community to assuage its feelings. In the face of such insensitivity, Hindu anger exploded into uncontrollable rage that spilled out onto the streets resulting in mad violence that should not have been. The anger was justified, the killings that followed were not.

A growing number of Hindus perceive that they have always been at the receiving end. Historical atrocities apart (hundreds of Hindu temples destroyed, thousands of Hindus killed or forcibly converted, imposition of religious taxes under Islamic rule), Hindus feel that it continues to the present day. In 1947, with the best of intentions, India's founding fathers rightly propounded a philosophy of secularism to protect the minority from majority domination and ensure equal rights for all. However, overzealous implementation deteriorated this policy into what is termed by Hindu groups as "an appeasement of the minorities."

According to this warped concept of secularism, regardless of the facts, the Hindu is always the perpetrator, and the Muslim the victim: a line blindly toed by the government, the media and, some feel, at times even the courts of law. A typical example of this is the plight of a quarter million Hindu refugees from Kashmir which evinces no reaction from the politically correct federal government or the so-called liberal media so as not to hurt the sentiments of the Muslims. Initially, Hindus took a back seat and refrained from any criticism of this attitude lest they be dubbed communal (a derogatory term in Indian lingo equivalent to a racist). But now many Hindus see this militant Hinduism as a bulwark against the growing Muslim fundamentalism that is engulfing South Asia.

A majority with a siege mentality may be difficult for a non-Indian to comprehend. Central to this is the Hindu theology of self-negation or sacrifice, at times carried to extreme lengths. In a land where

Mahatma Gandhi once brushed aside Hindu protests and offered the whole of India to Mr Jinnah, the leader of the Muslim League and the founder of Pakistan, and in a country where a hajj pilgrimage to Mecca is subsidized by the federal government (no such provision exists for the Hindu), one always wonders whether Hindu sentiments are dispensable. Things, however, are changing.

14

Godhra and its Aftermath:
A Dispassionate View

So much has happened and been said since that fateful morning in February* when a rail compartment full of Hindus was converted into an incinerator by a Muslim mob that one needs to step back and take a dispassionate and objective view of that horrific episode and the unruly events that followed. The views expressed during this sequence of events were totally at variance with each another. While the Gujarat government indicated it had done all that it could do to control the violence, the opposition spoke of deliberate stalling and even active encouragement of the mobs that went on an orgy of loot and murder. In this heated, emotion-driven environment, apart from human lives, truth, good sense and impartiality were also casualties.

While there is no denying the fact that the killings were barbaric in nature, the total lack of adherence to truth, disregard for impartiality, and exploitation across the board by political parties for their own petty, political ends has made solution of this problem extremely difficult, even impossible. In a society untoward incidents, though unfortunate, do occur, but a people are judged by their ability to tackle such events in a civilized fashion. Yes, there must be an inquiry, but by an impartial body. Street justice and trial by media are not the hallmarks of a civilized society or a democracy.

---

*   See chapter "Hindu Anger".

Inquiries by self-appointed guardians of our democracy who carry no moral authority or legal brief will not do. One such fact-finding mission[1] consisted of Dr Kamal Mitra Chenoy, Associate Professor, School of International Studies, Jawaharlal Nehru University, New Delhi; S. P. Shukla, IAS* (retd), former finance secretary to the Government of India and former member of the planning commission; K. S. Subramanian, IPS (retd), former director general of police, Tripura; and Achin Vanaik, Visiting Professor, Third World Academy, Jamia Millia Islamia, New Delhi. Let us see what they had to say.

This 'commission' found the following facts about the Godhra incident.

1) The Ram *sevaks* had not actually abducted a Muslim girl.

2) A mob of 2,000 Muslims did collect there in minutes.

3) GRP (Government Railway Police) did arrive on the site in a few minutes but made no effort to stop the mob.

4) An elected official actually stopped the firefighters from reaching the site.

Yet, the group concludes that this was not a premeditated act but a simple communal riot, as though there can be anything simple about an act that results in 59 humans being roasted alive.

In contrast to this conclusion, this self-appointed committee categorically states that the riots that followed were premeditated acts, carefully planned and systematically executed by the VHP and Bajrang Dal. But as one goes through the voluminous report carefully, one finds that there is not a shred of evidence to back up these claims. To support its charge that the rioters had lists of Muslim businesses, the group quotes a police circular issued in 1999. However, meticulous review of this circular suggests that the police were asked (in 1999, not recently) to keep track of Pakistani nationals and those Muslim organizations (not genuine businesses) that may be suspected of illegal

---

*   Indian Administrative Service, India's elite bureaucratic service.

activities. Nowhere is there an indication that ordinary Muslims were being targeted.

Such bodies are not fact-finding commissions dedicated to ascertaining the truth. They are not interested in proposing solutions to problems. These are witch-hunts orchestrated by bigoted groups consisting of individuals who flaunt impressive academic credentials but who will not hesitate to lie and distort facts in order to advance their own agenda.

Further, nearly every major English-language newspaper has written editorial after editorial demanding that Narendra Modi (chief minister of Gujarat) be dismissed for his handling of the Gujarat riots. The opposition parties and some of the NDA allies too have concurred with this view. Some noted jurists including Fali Nariman have joined this chorus. But let us a pause for a moment. Isn't a person innocent until proven guilty? Has any official body with authority deemed Modi guilty? Have the courts indicted him? Yes, hang Narendra Modi from the highest tree, but only when he is found guilty by an approved body. Trial by media that provides no recourse for defense is tantamount to lynching, which goes against the basic tenets of democracy.

Several important people have also not hesitated to point an accusing finger at the Gujarat government. Harsh Mander, an IAS officer, responded to the "call of his conscience" and resigned in protest against the Gujarat killings. But what bothers me is why this upright officer did not put in his papers when 3,000 Sikhs were burnt alive in Delhi in a pogrom (anti-Sikh Riots that followed Indira Gandhi's assassination in 1984) that was arguably condoned by the prime minister of the country at that time (Mr Rajiv Gandhi) and in which there was a clear case of delay in deploying the army?[2]

Similarly, when a retired admiral (who never raised his voice against the killings or harassment of Hindus in Kashmir) now writes a long-winded open letter to Prime Minister Atal Bihari Vajpayee expressing his anguish at the happenings in Gujarat, can I believe him?[3]

A doctoral candidate ensconced far away in a prestigious foreign university makes wild claims of organized violence, raves about the similarities between the *Hindutva* movement and Nazism, but fails to provide even an iota of proof. Mind you, all being said and done based on hearsay and even before any investigation has been conducted, so the reader can make his/her own judgment. I have always believed that it is the substance of the message that is important and not the messenger. The credentials of a person or his status in society hardly impress me. This episode has only served to strengthen my conviction and exposed the double standards, shallowness, and hypocrisy of some of our intelligentsia.

There was a lot of brouhaha about the purported statement made by Narendra Modi regarding a Newtonian law. Is this statement not similar to what Rajiv Gandhi (the then prime minister of India) allegedly said when his mother Mrs Gandhi was assassinated: "When a big tree falls, the earth will shake."[4] How much criticism did that statement evoke? It is such double standards that make me look with a cynical eye at the protestations of these individuals.

As opposed to these wild, sensational, fantasized opinions, presented below are some hard facts (backed by proof) which were presented by the Gujarat government and accepted by the NHRC (National Human Rights Commission) and the Minorities Commission (from *Outlook*). The NHRC and Minorities Commission have accepted the Gujarat government's contention that it did foresee trouble and took precautionary steps to check it, but was caught by surprise and overwhelmed by the mob fury erupting on February 28.

Now what actual measures did the Gujarat government take? The Gujarat government's own account given on March 5 is listed below, excerpted from an article by Prem Shanker Jha in *Outlook*.[5] He makes an important observation that this lacked the element of hindsight found in media reports.

> a) As soon as the seriousness of the Godhra incident became known, the state government immediately issued alert messages on February 27, 2002, to all district magistrates, commissioners and district superintendents of police. The administration was directed to exercise vigil and deal with anti-social and communal-minded elements firmly. Another alert message was issued the same day directing that preventive action be taken and adequate police *bandobast* (arrangements) maintained.

b) Further, the state government constantly reviewed the situation and decided to first call in additional central paramilitary forces on February 27, 2002, and thereafter the army on February 28, 2002. The state also requested additional forces from Madhya Pradesh, Maharashtra, and Rajasthan. Two companies of Maharashtra reserve police force arrived and were deployed in Surat. In addition, 66 companies of the SRP (State Reserve Police) were deployed immediately on February 27, 2002 itself.

c) As violence was reported on February 28, 2002, commissioners and superintendents of police were directed in no uncertain terms to take effective action to disperse unruly mobs. In fact, curfew was imposed in some affected parts of Ahmedabad on February 28 itself.

d) On March 1, 2002, which was Friday, the administration was alerted to keep peace and provide adequate *bandobast* to places of worship. On the same day (March 1), the police was instructed to implement riot control measures, enforce the curfew strictly, intensify patrolling, and take all necessary measures.

The next question we need to ask ourselves is whether these measures were actually taken. Or were these a litany of lies as alleged by some? Again, let us look at facts.[5] (Data given by the Gujarat police and accepted by the Minorities Commission.)

1) Till April 5, of 137 persons killed in police firing, 71 were Hindus. Of these, 90 had been killed by 6:00 AM on the morning of March 5.

2) By April 5, as many as 9,500 persons had been arrested of whom two-thirds were Hindus. Only 3,900 of these had been picked up in the first five days. This shows that the police continued to go after vandals and those it suspected of having participated in the looting, long after the actual violence had died down.

So when one looks at the Gujarat riots shorn of the emotional hoopla, one comes up with a different picture. On March 6, 2002, the Government of Gujarat announced the setting up of a one-man commission headed by retired Justice K. G. Shah to look into the communal violence in Gujarat. Like a civilized society which abides by rules and regulations, we must await the findings of this commission and then form opinions and take appropriate action, according to the stipulations of our democracy.

15

Hindu Temples in the Age of Pseudo-Secularism

My mother has always been of a religious bent of mind. Every morning after her customary bath, she recites her usual prayers and sets aside a small amount of money in a crumpled plastic wrapper which she keeps tucked away in one corner of our modest *puja* [prayer] room, a practice carried on unfailingly for over 40 years. At the end of the month or at some later time, she takes the money and deposits it in the *hundi* [donation box] at the Radhakrishna temple near our house in India. When she happens to be out of the country for extended periods of time, she uses the postal service to send her donations to our ancestral temple in a remote part of northern Karnataka, or on occasion to "Venkappa" (Shri Venkateswara of Tirupati), as she calls him.

Then there is Krishnabehn (name changed), the middle-aged lady from rural Gujarat who ekes out a modest living by cooking at our home on weekdays and working in a warehouse on weekends. I was somewhat surprised when she mentioned the monetary amount (a significant chunk of her salary) she routinely donates to the mandir.

I cite these two incidents to underline the purity of thought and specificity of purpose that underlie this giving. The fact that these two pious women, like millions of others, channel their charity through a temple has certain implications. They desire that their efforts go to sustain Hindu temples and be used expressly for Hindu charitable causes. But does this really happen? A few are quick to retort that middlemen siphon off large amounts—a distinct possibility. But my focus in this article is on the role of the government and the dubious manner in which it handles these donations. Is it transparent and in keeping with the intentions of these devotees? And the more germane query is: should the government even be in this business?

At present, most Hindu temples in the states of Karnataka, Kerala, and Tamil Nadu are under the jurisdiction of the government. In addition, prominent temples in other parts of the country like Jagannath Puri, Tirupati, Kashi Vishwanath, Vaishno Devi, Guruvayoor, Chamunda Devi, Dattapeeth, Kali Mandir of Patiala, Amarnath, Badrinath, and Kedarnath are administered by government-appointed bodies. Moving a step ahead, in 2004, the UPA government made a proposal to a parliamentary standing committee to acquire all Hindu temples and levy a tax on their earnings.

This is faulty on two accounts. First, it goes against the basic tenet of secularism that dictates non-interference by the state in religious matters. Second, this decision smacks of blatant discrimination. When other religions like Islam and Christianity are given total freedom to conduct their affairs, why should Hinduism alone be singled out for these restrictive regulations?

In a landmark decision on September 9, 2006, the Karnataka High Court struck down the Karnataka Hindu Religious and Endowment Act of 1997 indicating that "the legislation violated Articles 14, 25 and 26 of the Constitution which provided for right to equality, freedom of conscience and freedom of profession, practice and propagation of religion and also the freedom to manage the religious affairs."[1]

Ideological objections are only one part of the story. Practical interference appears to be crafted to benefit other religions at the expense of Hindu interests, a process facilitated by partisan politics. Some figures that give a clearer picture of this subtle embezzlement follow.

In 1997, the Karnataka government received a revenue of over Rs. 52 crore (1 crore is equal to 10 million) rupees from 264,000 Hindu temples. While 17 crores were returned to the temples for maintenance, *Rs. 12 crores was diverted to support madrassas* and churches.* The balance of 23 crores was usurped by the government for its own programs. The figures for 1998 were similar.

By 1999, one notices that the disparity widens, with less being retained for Hindu temples and more being allocated to Muslim and Christian institutions. Of the 65 crores collected, a meager 15 was given back to temples, with 27 and 8 crores being reserved for *madrassas* and church development respectively. The remainder was unaccounted for. With the trend continuing, Hindu temples received only 10 crores of their 72 crore revenue in 2002 with *madrassas* pocketing a whopping 50 crores and Christians making away with 10 crores.[2]

These statistics prove to be even more damning when this chicanery is viewed against the backdrop of the 50,000 or so of 260,000 Hindu temples in Karnataka that lie in a state of abject neglect throughout the length and breadth of this state: *pujas* are not performed daily, salaries are not disbursed on time, and priests subsist on handouts by devotees. In short, while hundreds of Hindu temples languish untended, money that the poorest of Hindus sacrifice and offer for upkeep of their temples and subsistence of their faith is being used to garnish Muslim mosques and Christian churches: a shocking travesty of justice.

These data raise two pertinent questions. Does the government have the right to use religious money for secular purposes? Can money from Hindu charities be diverted to Muslim and Christian bodies without the consent of the former, and can or will the reverse be done?

Answers to both these questions have distinct legal implications, a fact confirmed by the recent ruling of the Karnataka High Court against the Karnataka Hindu Religious and Endowment Act of 1997. Castigating this illegal siphoning off of funds, the court categorically decreed, "Devotees of Hindu temples provide money for temple purposes and it cannot be spent for non-Hindu causes."***

---

*   Islamic religious schools.
*   Islamic religious schools.

Throughout the ages, Hindu temples, because of their magnificence and opulence have always evoked ire, envy, and greed leading at times to their eventual destruction. The early part of the second millennium saw Muslims loot, plunder, and raze thousands of Hindu temples. In modern times, Hindu temples are not being physically destroyed: they are being economically bled to death by unprincipled governments pursuing a warped policy.

16

Indian Intellectuals: A Failure to Lead

The intellectual community is supposed to be the friend, philosopher and guide to the nation. Supposedly endowed with superior intellect, the nation looks up to this body of individuals to provide an insightful and accurate analysis of crucial events that aid the betterment of the nation. But like the kitten that finds itself entangled in a bundle of wool unable to extricate itself, our intelligentsia lies trapped in a psychological quagmire of its own making unable to perform any useful function. Dictated by narrow ideologies in lieu of factual evidence, it is a confused body that is incapable of seeing the larger picture or defining the true destiny of the nation. In short, in the battle against terrorism, our intelligentsia has proved to be more of a distraction sometimes with a deliberate intent to misguide, as coverage of the Mumbai blasts˙ indicate.

By their writings in editorials and columns of leading newspapers, these scribes, instead of presenting the nation with a meticulous exposition of the issue with possible solutions, have shown themselves to be ardent apologists for the terrorists, supplying them with ample reasons to justify their ghastly attacks.

---

*   On July 11, 2006 (or 7/11) a series of terrorist bombs ripped through seven commuter trains in Mumbai killing over two hundred people.

Time and again, Gujarat 2002 has been held up as the sentinel event that is the genesis of terrorism in India. An editorial in the *Indian Express* (July 14, 2006) claimed: "The Gujarat riots of 2002 stoked deep-seated resentments in local Muslim communities that jihadi outfits—which earlier given much less quarter—could exploit for their own nefarious purposes."

Again holding communal riots to be the instigating factor, Muzamil Jaleel in an op-ed[1] in the same newspaper remarks:

> Chand Khan—the man who ferried fidayeens from South Kashmir to Akshardham—had told his interrogators in Srinagar that he joined the jihadi group only after [the] Gujarat riots. Azam Ghauri's evolution in becoming one of India's most wanted militants has its roots in communal riots. According to the investigations, Ghauri—who had a Naxal past—was present at a meeting organised in Bhiwandi soon after communal violence had ripped it apart in 1985. Then there is Jalees Ansari—a doctor who was arrested in 1994. He decided to leave his job and plant bombs on December 6, 1992—the day of the Babri demolition. Ansari joined the Tehreek-Islahul-Muslimeen (Movement for Reform among Muslims)—an extremist group founded in Mominpura (Mumbai) to "avenge" communal violence against Muslims.

These conclusions are flawed, to say the least. First, to postulate a direct linear relationship between a perceived injustice or communal riots and terrorism is surely naive. The Hindu relatives of the Godhra victims did not heed a call to terror. Seething in a cauldron of injustice, deprivation and suppression, a potent recipe for terror, the internally displaced Kashmiri Hindus should have spawned numerous terror groups. That did not happen.

Second, what sort of warped logic is this? One wrong does not nullify another or mitigate the magnitude of a crime, period, let us be clear about that. This is a precept that even the common man on the street understands: how it fails these so-called intellectuals I find it hard to comprehend. If the ghost of Gujarat 2002 can be invoked to justify every subsequent terrorist act or the foray of Indian Muslims into terrorism, then by the same token, the slaughter at Noakhali* or the carnage of Somnath can be used to rationalize not one but a hundred Gujarats.

Moreover, such a claim does not even conform to a logical sequence. The Kandahar** hijacking and the sensational assault on our Parliament both preceded Gujarat 2002. Let us not make excuses for a crime that is innately evil.

In addition to propagating a cause-and-effect theory, these so-called intellectuals make every attempt to temper these savage acts by unjust comparisons and willful distraction in order to alter public perception of these events.

An example of this is the layout of the op-ed page of the *Indian Express* dated July 25, 2006. In the centre of the article (an interview of K. P. S. Gill by Shekhar Gupta on the Naxal threat) is an outsized image of Gill, the security icon and archenemy of terrorists who is credited with putting down the Sikh insurgency. What is even more striking is the caption splashed boldly across the entire page above the picture: "The only time I've slept badly in my life was in Gujarat. Just hearing the descriptions. Never before, never after."

How this headline is relevant to the topic of the interview (the Naxal threat) escapes me, initially, that is. A little thought makes the intention clearer. With the country still recovering from the Mumbai blasts of just a week earlier and the focus squarely on the Islamic community, how else do you deflect the scrutiny: resurrect Gujarat 2002.

Naresh Fernandes, while writing in the *New York Times* on the Mumbai bomb blasts, finds it imperative to pull the "Hindu Shiv Sena" into the picture, never mind the irrelevance or the insignificance of the protest: no lives were lost in the protest, he highlights. He graphically comments:

---

*   Noakhali, now in Bangladesh was the scene of a horrific massacre of Hindus in 1946 with the death toll estimated in thousands.

**   The hijack of an Indian Airlines plane to Kandahar in Afghanisthan by Islamic militants in 1999.

As we settled down to brunch on Sunday, our TV sets brought us the chilling sight of buses being ransacked and burnt across Mumbai by cadres of the Hindu nativist Shiv Sena party. They claimed that a statue of their leader's late wife had been vandalized, and they were protesting in the only way they knew how.[2]

Lacking the courage to target the real culprits or the acumen to perform a critical analysis, pseudo-intellectuals use these acts of terrorism to sermonize the Hindu community instead. Sudheendra Kulkarni comments:

> But 7/11 has a lesson for the Hindu community too. Quite often in the past, some Hindu organizations have fallen to the provocation. They too haven't done enough, and honest enough, self-introspection. They think that Hindu fanaticism, which was responsible for the barbaric post-Godhra violence in Gujarat, is the answer to Muslim fanaticism. They routinely feed anti-Muslim prejudices, or at least condone those who do so. They know not the disservice they are doing to India, and to themselves.[3]

Carefully dissect this excerpt to fully realize the undiluted hypocrisy and double standards that have become the hallmark of the Indian intellectual scene, an inspiring doctrine for continued Islamic terrorism in India. The Gujarat riots are cited to justify Mumbai 7/11, but a similar correlation between Godhra (Hindu victims) and Gujarat 2002 escapes the writer. While the post-Godhra riots are described as barbaric, the Godhra incident itself, in which 59 Hindu men, women, and children were roasted alive to the taunts of a jeering mob, is conveniently overlooked, a deliberate attempt at obfuscation.

Coming back to the crux of the matter: you can crucify Modi for Gujarat 2002, you can pontificate endlessly on the nonexistent bogey of Hindu fanaticism and claim perfidiously that Hindus were the first suicide bombers, or that other groups are equally guilty of such heinous crimes, but does any of this provide a solution to the problem? No. And therein lies the greatest failure of the Indian intelligentsia: a lack of clear thinking and an inability to lead.

17

The Miracle that is India

Growing up in the southern city of Bangalore in the early 1970s, I was appalled to see differing political factions of Iranian students indulging in open street fights. What an uncultured group these people are, I thought. It was a classic example of washing one's dirty linen in public in a different country. It evoked disgust. It is the same feeling that I sense, here in New York, when I view the local *desi* [native] scene in the context of the denial of a U.S. visa to Narendra Modi, Chief Minister of Gujarat (a western Indian state). I do not wish to dwell on the pros and cons of the issue, but to analyze what such episodes do to our image as a nation and a people. How does it reflect upon of all of us, the secular groups, the nationalist factions or whatever (I hate these labels for they mislead)? Is this the right forum to wash our dirty linen? Does it serve any purpose apart from demoralizing us?

We as a nation appear to be excessively obsessed about how we are perceived. What will the world think of us is the question we often ask ourselves and is a mantra that is chanted again and again. Now who or what is this "world" that we keep referring to? Is it the Western governments? The Western media? Or the public in these countries? And how is this opinion shaped? Does it stem from independent judgment? Or is it a reflection of how we project ourselves?

During colonial times the British encouraged an unsavory image of India in order to justify their rule: the natives are unfit to rule themselves, was their premise. According to them, snake charmers, emaciated cows on the streets and ubiquitous dirt seemed to embody India, prompting even Mahatma Gandhi to dub such descriptions as nothing more than "a drain inspector's report." Writing in *Young India*, Mahatma Gandhi said:

> [Katherine Mayo's book *Mother India*] is the report of a drain inspector sent out with one purpose of opening and examining the drains of the country to be reported upon.... If Miss Mayo had confessed that she had gone to India merely to open out and examine the drains of India, there would be little to complain about her compilation. But she says, in effect, with a certain amount of triumph "*the drains are India.*"

As these stereotyped images of India conjured up during colonial times fade away today, another, uglier and more repulsive than the previous, is being created. Events are being exaggerated or blown out of proportion in order to sensationalize news items and thereby make them more appealing to Western audiences. However, the culprits this time are not the West or Europeans. The detractors are our own homegrown writers enthusiastically misusing a new-found access to the world stage with each one trying to outdo the other in this calumny.

Pankaj Mishra is the author of the novel, *The Romantics* and a regular contributor to the *New York Times*. On the eve of Clinton's visit to India in March 2000, in a scene that conformed to a Nazi how-to manual, 33 Sikhs are rounded up and gunned down in cold blood by Islamic militants. The hideous crime shocks the nation and reverberates throughout the world. But Pankaj Mishra chooses to see it differently. In an article titled, "Pride and Blood in Kashmir" (*New York Times*, March 22, 2000), he uses this barbaric act, not to castigate the militants for their brutality, but to censure the Indian government for its high-handedness. He quotes a Border Security Force person who tells him, "I don't believe in this human rights nonsense." Pankaj Mishra concludes, "The military arms of all-powerful authorities in New Delhi have been used to suppress regional discontent." In effect, he is telling the outside world that Indian democracy is a sham.

In another article ("Hinduism's Political Resurgence," *New York Times*, February 25, 2002), Mishra goes a step further, preferring

Pakistan under the dictator Musharraf to democratic India under the BJP: "While General Musharraf strives toward a secular polity, the ruling politicians of India head in the opposite direction." Imagine the irony when he surmises: "Oddly, the illiberal tendencies a military dictator seeks to expel, with popular support, from Pakistan seem to be finding a hospitable home in democratic India."

These writers are at their worst or best (from their perspective) when they report on anything to do with Hindu nationalism. Reproduced below is a paragraph from Mishra's, "The Other Face of Fanaticism" (*New York Times*, February 2, 2003). Referring to the Gujarat violence, he writes:

> The scale of the violence was matched only by its brutality. Women were gang-raped before being killed. Children were burned alive. Grave-diggers at mass burial sites told investigators "that most bodies that had arrived ... were burned and butchered beyond recognition. Many were missing body parts—arms, legs and even heads. The elderly and the handicapped were not spared.

Is this the image of India that we wish to project to the outside world? Again am I saying: hush up these evil acts? No. Use the right forums to seek redress if that is your real intention. Do not sensationalize events to garner personal glory.

A. Ghosh's report in *Time* ("Subcontinental Drift: Fear Over the City," March 7, 2002) is along the same lines. He speaks of how people boasted of the killings associated with the Gujarat riots and adds:

> Some, if not all, of this was undoubtedly pure braggadocio. The stories sounded fake, or at least embellished for effect. "It was like a bunch of schoolboys boasting about imaginary achievements," said my friend. "But these so-called achievements were murderous." What was especially scary was the casual, matter-of-fact tone in which this conversation was conducted. "These guys seemed no more agitated than they would have if they were talking about the weather," said my friend. It was like an everyday discussion.

If Ghosh realizes that these incidents are not entirely true (embellished for effect) and suggestive of "pure braggadocio" as he himself puts it, why does he feel the need to document them, especially in an international magazine? Apart from netting him a byline and falsely maligning Indians, does it serve any function?

Look how Meenaksi Ganguly writing in *Time* ("In the Heart of Hate," March 11, 2002) uses one man's words to denigrate the Hindus as a whole:

> Another man boasted that he had killed nine Muslims. "I was acting for all Hindus," he said.

Their writing is graphic in a most negative way and meant to portray the worst of India. Read this excerpt from Shashi Tharoor's article, paying close attention to the words I have italicized ("India's Past Becomes a Weapon," *New York Times*, March 6, 2002):

> In 1992 a *howling mob of Hindu extremists* tore down the Babri Masjid, which occupied a prominent spot in a town otherwise overflowing with temples. The mosque had been built in the 1520s by India's first Mogul emperor, Babur; the Hindu *zealots* vowed to replace it with a temple to Ram. In other words, they want to *avenge* history by undoing the shame of half a millennium ago.

Such writings effectively conjure up an image of a country filled with bloodthirsty religious fanatics.

As these articles indicate, most articles about India appearing in the foreign news media are penned by Indians or people of Indian origin. During the months of March–April, 2002, the *Washington Post* had 12 reports (most of them not complimentary) on the Gujarat riots: six were by Rama Lakshmi, five by Rajiv Chandrasekaran and one by Salman Rushdie.

In the debate about Gujarat, Indian newspapers are extremely fond of referencing an "international" organization; the New York–based Human Rights Watch. But do you know who authored the report on Gujarat put out by HRW? Smitha Narula, a person of Indian origin.

So an objective evaluation reveals that what we perceive as "Western opinion" is really not so. It is, in fact, a veneer that has been deviously crafted by Indian political groups pursuing a narrow agenda.

What makes these Indian writers depict India in this fashion? Two reasons. One is that the Western public (like the public everywhere) craves melodrama which these Indian writers are ever willing to provide even at the cost of truth and honesty. The urge to "get published" in the Western press drives them to dramatize events. Second, this is ideological warfare being waged by the Indian left against the Hindu right. Unfortunately, the so-called liberal wing in India has a large cadre of well-educated (though not intellectual) Westernized journalists who are able to interact with their counterparts in the West and thereby propagate their one-sided views.

Compared to the pessimism that pervades the writings of Indian authors, Western writers tend to be more fair and balanced about India. Reproduced below is an abstract from an op-ed piece, "Vote France Off the Island" (*New York Times*, February 9, 2003) by noted columnist Thomas Friedman.

> Sometimes I wish that the five permanent members of the U.N. Security Council could be chosen like the starting five for the N.B.A. All-Star team—with a vote by the fans. If so, I would certainly vote France off the Council and replace it with India. Then the perm-five would be Russia, China, India, Britain and the United States. That's more like it.
>
> Why replace France with India? Because India is the world's biggest democracy, the world's largest Hindu nation and the world's second-largest Muslim nation, and, quite frankly, India is just so much more serious than France these days. France is so caught up with its need to differentiate itself from America to feel important, it's become silly. India has grown out of that game. India may be ambivalent about war in Iraq, but it comes to its ambivalence honestly. Also, France can't see how the world has changed since the end of the cold war. India can.

In another article, "Where Freedom Reigns" (*New York Times*, August 14, 2002) Friedman concludes:

> The more time you spend in India the more you realize that this teeming, multiethnic, multireligious, multilingual country is one

of the world's great wonders—a miracle with a message. And the message is that democracy matters.

This truth hits you from every corner. Consider Bangalore, where the traffic is now congested by all the young Indian techies, many from the lower-middle classes, who have gotten jobs, apartments—and motor scooters—by providing the brainpower for the world's biggest corporations. While the software designs of these Indian techies may be rocket science, what made Bangalore what it is today is something very simple: 50 years of Indian democracy and secular education, and 15 years of economic liberalization, produced all this positive energy.

Even when commenting about something unpleasant like the Hindu-Muslim riots of Gujarat, a foreigner like Friedman is willing to analyze events objectively. His observations are tempered with good sense and good judgment. Though critical of the riots and the Hindu nationalist BJP, he is reluctant to demonize events. His keen journalistic eye observes that the riots did not spread to other parts of India—as one would expect.

No, India is not paradise. Just last February the Hindu nationalist B.J.P. government in the state of Gujarat stirred up a pogrom by Hindus against Muslims that left 600 Muslims, and dozens of Hindus, dead. It was a shameful incident, and in a country with 150 million Muslims—India has the largest Muslim minority in the world—it was explosive. And do you know what happened? Nothing happened. The rioting didn't spread anywhere.

So am I saying that violent crimes and brutal injustice should be hushed up or swept under the rug? That a foreigner's view is more important than an Indian's? No, on both accounts. My only grouse is with the forum that one uses for this purpose. Such exposure on the international front hardly serves any constructive purpose. The world is not going to shower accolades on us for washing our dirty linen in public. It will only use this information to chastise us and imply obliquely that we are not yet ready to be granted a permanent seat in the UN. Further, it tends to strengthen colonial notions of Indians as

'uncivilized natives' incapable of resolving their problems in a sophisticated manner.

All said and done, India still boasts of an infrastructure that works.
Our courts do hand out fair judgments. Our newspapers possess a
degree of freedom that is unmatched in the world. That this freedom
has been blatantly misused in recent times is another story. More
importantly, we have a functioning parliament that allows every griev-
ance to be voiced publicly. So if one genuinely desires redress without ulterior motives, these are avenues that can be tapped and should
be. Recourse to the world stage is relevant only in cases of suppressed
nations—which India is not.

18

Freedom of Religion and Conversion Not Synonymous

"The Indian sub-continent with one billion people is a living example of what happens when Satan rules the entire culture.... India is one vast purgatory in which millions of people ... are literally living a cosmic lie! Could Satan have devised a more perfect system for causing misery?" (Gospel for Asia, Texas)*

In what seemed more like a directive rather than a comment, Pope Benedict, the newly-anointed Pope of Christendom, told Amitava Tripathi, India's ambassador to the Vatican in June 2006, that "the disturbing signs of religious intolerance which have troubled some regions of the nation, including the reprehensible attempt to legislate clearly discriminatory restrictions on the fundamental right of religious freedom, must be firmly rejected." Continuing his homily, he sermonized, "... anti-conversion laws were unconstitutional (and) contrary to the highest ideals of India's founding fathers."

This self-righteous hectoring about religious bigotry coming from the head of a Church that was the proponent of the deadly Inquisition in Europe (and closer to home in Goa) in the Middle Ages and which was an enthusiastic cheerleader for the fanatic rampage of the Spanish conquistadores in South America and is guided by principles like those

---

*   Arun Shourie, *Missionaries in India.*

in quotes above, must certainly appear strange. The Pope's assertion reveals a profound misunderstanding of the ideals espoused by our founding fathers and the principles enshrined in our traditions.

By these remarks, Pope Benedict appears to have picked up from where his predecessor left off. The late Pope John Paul II was also a fervent champion of proselytization. On a visit to India in 1991, he showed scant respect for Hindu sentiments by giving a universal call for conversion on Diwali day, one of Hinduism's holiest days. To add fuel to the fire, he followed it up with distasteful remarks critical of India's anti-conversion laws that had been passed in some Indian states. He commented: "Unfortunately, in some regions (of India) the state authorities have yielded to the pressures of these extremists (read Hindu nationalist groups) and have passed unjust conversion laws, prohibiting free exercise of the natural right to religious freedom, or withdrawing state support for those in the scheduled castes who have chosen Christianity."

The use of the words "extremists" and "scheduled castes" suggest a sinister political design aimed at exploiting the weaker sections of the Hindu society and creating dissension among its ranks for the express purpose of conversion.

And the repeated emphasis on "free exercise of the natural right to religious freedom" (Pope John Paul) and "fundamental right of religious freedom" (Pope Benedict) is nothing more than camouflage for aggressive proselytization. One must understand that freedom of religion is one thing, active conversion another. It would be erroneous to equate one with the other. Freedom of religion means that a person can of one's own free will accept another religion if one is disillusioned with one's own or if one finds the teachings of another more satisfying spiritually. But note that it must be totally of one's own free will; there must be no force, no propaganda, and above all there must be no inducement, financial or material. The Supreme Court of India concurs with this definition. In a landmark judgment on September 2, 2003, the court said it must be remembered that Article 25(1) "… postulates that there is no fundamental right to convert another person to one's own religion because if a person purposely undertakes the conversion of another person to his religion, that would impinge on the freedom of conscience guaranteed to all the citizens of the country alike."

Indians (or Hindus in particular) have no argument with the intellectual freedom of individuals when it comes to religion. Gautama Buddha turned away from Hinduism to propound his own teachings, yet is revered in every Hindu home in India. Their grouse is with the nefarious, underhand tactics adopted by non-Hindu religions that have turned religion from being a process of moral advancement into a political game of numbers.

Conversion has always been anathema to the Hindu mind because unlike other religions, Hinduism has never claimed an exclusive right to divinity. The ability to realize that there could be more than one way to God has pervaded our scriptures for centuries. *Truth is one; the wise call it by different names* is an old quote from the Vedas.

Mahatma Gandhi writing in *Young India* (January 19, 1928) said: "I came to the conclusion long ago, after prayerful search and study and discussion with as many people as I could meet, that all religions are true, and also that all had some error in them, and whilst I hold my own, I should hold others as dear as Hinduism...."

In another message he concludes, "It was impossible for me to believe that I could go to heaven or attain salvation only by becoming a Christian...."

When one is willing to concede that all religions are equal, then the concept of conversion becomes redundant. Conversion represents a retreat in the course of man's spiritual progress. Vivekananda, addressing the World's Parliament of Religions in Chicago in 1893 asserted:

> Do I wish that the Christian would become Hindu? God forbid. Do I wish that the Hindu or Buddhist would become Christian? God forbid. The seed is put in the ground and earth and air and water are placed around it. Does the seed become the earth or the air or the water? No. It becomes a plant, it develops after the law of its own growth, assimilates the air, the earth, and the water, converts them into plant substance and grows into a plant. Similar is the case with religion. The Christian is not to become a Hindu or a Buddhist, nor a Hindu or a Buddhist to become a

Christian. But each must assimilate the spirit of the other and grow according to his own law of growth.

Gandhi's views on conversion were equally blunt and direct. Without mincing words, he wrote, "I disbelieve in the conversion of one person by another. My effort should never be to undermine another's faith but to make him a better follower of his own faith. This implies the belief in the truth of all religions and respect for them."

The Church and so-called secular groups have often decried anti-conversion bills and ascribed their passage to the machinations of the Sangh Parivar. However, I would like the reader to pause for a moment and read the quotes[1] below.

"But no propaganda can be allowed which reviles other religions. For that would be negation of toleration. The best way of dealing with such propaganda is to publicly condemn it."

"If I had the power and could legislate, I should stop all proselytizing."

"It is no use trying to fight these forces without giving up the idea of conversion, which I assure you is the deadliest poison that ever sapped the fountain of truth."

Do you know who wrote these words? Not Guru Golwalkar, the patriarch of the RSS, not Praveen Togadia, the firebrand leader of the VHP. It was Mahatma Gandhi and, if he were alive today he would have given unwavering support to this decree. The anti-conversion laws carry with them the spiritual might of the Mahatma. Are our so-called secularists aware of Gandhi's views on conversion? Or are they conveniently using only those teachings of Gandhi that suit their warped political agenda?

So what do we do now? How does India as a nation address this issue of religious conversion? How can India maintain the delicate balance between its myriad religious communities and continue its long tradition of religious tolerance? There is only one panacea. Prohibit all conversions: even better, if the Christians and Muslims of India voluntarily give up all proselytization and proscribe terms like "heathen" and "kafir" from their religious books. Is that too much to ask? Aggressive proselytization can only serve to disturb the religious ecology and create discord between people. Conversion is the raison d'être for the distrust between religions. In the absence of this contentious issue, religions will be able to coexist.

Maintenance of religious harmony is the responsibility of one and all. Mutual respect for each other's religion is essential for this. So far, Hinduism has shown exemplary restraint by not pointing a finger at other religions or exploiting their failings to further itself; even the most rabid Hindu groups adhere to this principle. They are only involved in protecting their own rights.

In contrast, other religions have repeatedly used devious means to defame and denigrate Hinduism. Take the case of the Jhajjar incident that occurred a few years ago. What happened in Jhajjar when five Dalits were lynched is disgusting and needs to be condemned by one and all. However, do you know what the Christians and Muslims did? They rushed to Jhajjar, not to console the community, but to incite them to convert. Is this not fishing in troubled waters? Is this justified? Certainly not.

One must remember that there are skeletons in everyone's closets. Using the same modus operandi, Hindus could focus on the deficiencies of other religions to castigate them. This, however, does not conform to the enlightened wisdom of Hinduism. And I also know that it is wrong to tarnish these great religions (Christianity and Islam) because of the misdeeds of a few. By the same token Christianity and Islam must learn not to exploit the inadequacies of Hinduism for their own narrow ends. My reason for this retort is not to hurt anyone's sentiments but to convey a message in no uncertain terms: If you want us to respect your religion, you must learn to respect ours. There are no two ways about it.

Finally, I pose the question: How should Hindus react to this onslaught on their community? Though theologically inconsistent with Hindu values, should Hindu religious leaders endorse conversion and actively propagate Hinduism? The VHP has a *ghar vapasi* (return home) program, but I am speaking of a massive movement sanctioned by all Hindu religious leaders. Is this not more pragmatic? Will it not be a politically astute move and evoke an effective response?

19

The Sachar Report: An Objective Analysis

(The Sachar Report, submitted to the Indian Parliament in November 2006, was a government-sponsored exercise specifically aimed at providing the UPA [Congress party and its allies] with a justification to provide sops to the Muslims in return for votes.)

Statistics are akin to snapshots: they capture a flash in time. Statistics cast little light on the antecedents or the etiologic factors that conspired to produce those precise numbers. Faced with inane numbers, the human mind can analyze the data accurately, objectively, and intelligently, or indulge in a whimsical fantasy that furthers one's prejudged opinions. The media's treatment of the Sachar Report qualifies as naive credulity at best or devious machination at worst.

Methodology or the manner in which the statistics are compiled in a survey is crucial. Was the Sachar Report a scientifically conducted independent exercise conforming to the rules of statistics (no bias) and aimed at arriving at an accurate picture? Did this report accurately survey the entire Muslim population or a representative cross-section of that community? The answer is in the negative. These data were obtained by visiting a few selected states and interviewing select institutions like government agencies, NGOs, and Muslim organizations, an approach with a definite propensity for bias. Justice Sachar, himself acutely aware of these deficiencies of his report, cautions: "These figures are based on what people and organizations told us when we met them in the states. They need to be analyzed before arriving at any final conclusion." So, far from being an accurate reflection of society, the Sachar Report appears to be a mish-mash of numbers hastily collected with a political intent in mind but with dangerous ramifications for Indian society and the country as a whole.

Despite its shortcomings, the Sachar Report when reviewed meticulously fails to substantiate the charges doing the media rounds or corroborate the inferences drawn by so-called intellectuals and vested political interests. Let us look carefully at the data as they pertain to charges of discrimination, the extent of Muslim poverty, and the adequacy of education available to the children in this community.

Discrimination

When the proportion of a community in government jobs does not mirror their percentage in the population, can it be automatically assumed that this stems from blatant prejudice? Definitely not, as various reasons could have contributed to the outcome. For one, the age distribution among Muslims is lopsided, with a distinct shift to the left (higher percentage less than 18 years), leading to a definite contraction in the job-seeking subset. While this can be dismissed as extrapolated information or speculative conjecture, there is an additional factor that is more tangible and which directly correlates with this disturbing finding: the paucity of qualified persons in this community.

According to the report, only 3.2 percent of Muslims aged 20 and over are graduates compared to the national average of 6.7 percent, which clearly diminishes the appropriately qualified applicant pool among Muslims. Sunil Jain clearly points this out in *Business Standard* (December 2, 2006).

> The fact is that despite the high-decibel campaign launched by the media on leaks from the Sachar Committee Report, as in the case of the OBCs, there is no sign of any systemic discrimination against the Muslims when it comes to jobs; the problem lies in the enrolment levels of Muslims in schools. The 1999–2000 NSS data show, for instance, that while Muslims comprised 12.2 per

cent of the country's population, their share in those who had passed school was just 7.2 per cent. The rest then follows from this number—so, the Muslims formed just 6.5 per cent of the proportion of those enrolled in college, though they still managed to get 9.7 percent of the total number of "professional, technical and managerial" jobs in the country.

Sensational and shoddy reporting associated with the Sachar Report abound. A leading newspaper (*Indian Express*, December 3, 2006) titles an article with an eye-catching headline, "Muslims Discriminated," and goes on to reference this statement of the Sachar Committee: "Muslim workers are paid less than their counterparts from other communities owing to the nature and skill of the work they do." Continuing, the article cites the reason for this difference, again quoting from the Sachar Report: "A large part of the difference is likely to be due to the nature of the private sector enterprises themselves, with the Muslims being engaged in smaller and informal jobs and thereby low-productivity enterprises."

Is this discrimination? Muslims are being paid different amounts because as the report itself acknowledges, they perform "smaller and informal jobs." This is not differential treatment. Discrimination can be inferred when two people with equal qualifications are paid different amounts for the *same type of work*, e.g., two physicians performing exactly the same work. But if a physician and a hospital orderly (each belonging to a different religion) were paid different amounts taking into consideration the nature of duties, it would be ridiculous to infer discrimination. Apples cannot be compared to oranges.

Poverty

Selective data culled from the Sachar Report have been provocatively highlighted to project the Muslims as an economically deprived community in comparison with other sections of society. Careful scrutiny of the data reveals a picture more gray in appearance than one distinctly divided into black and white.

Poverty is quantified by several direct measures like the per capita income and the Mean Per Capita Expenditure (MPCE) which defines the consumption expenditure of individuals. The poverty ratio or Head Count Ratio (HCR) estimates the percentage of those whose consumption is below the poverty line, an index that stood at Rs. 328 in rural areas and Rs. 454 in urban areas at last count in 1999–2000 and which signifies the rupee value of basic nutritional requirement.

The all-India average for the MPCE (Sachar Report) was Rs. 712. The figures for Muslims were 636, for OBCs' 645, and SC/STs'' 520. The MPCE for Muslims is only Rs. 76 off the national average, amounting to a negligible difference of Rs. 2.50 per day—not something earth-shattering as some of columnists have been making it out to be. Further, by this criterion, Muslims are better off than SC/STs (31 percent of Hindus) and almost on par with OBCs (43 percent of Hindus): certainly not at the bottom of the heap.

When evaluated by HCR, a slightly different picture emerges. In 2004–5, the overall HCR for the country was 22.7 percent with individual figures for SC/STs, Muslims, and OBCs being 35, 31, and 21 percent respectively. While SC/STs continue to flounder at the bottom, OBCs do much better than Muslims (a difference of 10 percent) by this parameter.

As these figures are further analyzed taking into account geographic location, the picture for Muslims does not appear dismal in the least. The HCR for rural Muslims was 26.9 percent vs. a national average of 22.7 percent, a difference that does not meet the test of statistical significance. But what was even more striking was that *Muslims were more affluent* than the combined Hindu community in 10 of the 21 states surveyed by the Sachar Commission and, in Tamil Nadu, Muslims even outdid the Hindu upper castes in terms of economic prosperity. Additionally, for the period 1993–4 to 2004–5, rural Muslims recorded the highest rate of economic growth with an HCR drop of 12 percent compared to an 8 percent decline for Hindus. This clearly suggests that the rural Muslims at least are not a disadvantaged lot in comparison to other socio-religious groups.

---

*   Other Backward Classes.
**   Scheduled Castes/Scheduled Tribes.

Urban Muslims, on the contrary, do come out poorly with an HCR of 38.4 percent, with SC/STs close on their heels at 36.4 percent. Urban Muslim poverty matched that of Hindus in only 4 of the 21 states.

Let me quote data from another source to indicate that Muslims are not the only underprivileged lot. According to a more scientifically done study (J. Radhakrishna, *Brahmins of India*, Allahabad: Chugh Publications), 55 percent of the Brahmins (upper castes) in a district of Andhra Pradesh live below the poverty line compared to a national average of 45 percent at that time. This is not an isolated instance of Brahmin penury. Brahmins in Karnataka register a per capita income of Rs. 537 compared to a figure of Rs. 794 for Muslims.[1]

By deliberately using the Brahmin community (the so-called most privileged of the Hindus) as an example I wish to emphasize that traditional concepts no longer hold water in a fast-changing India. The face of poverty is rapidly changing. Poverty in India is a hydra-headed monster which spreads its tentacles erratically clasping one community in one area and a different one in another. No one community is immune.

To claim that it is the exclusive curse of one community or region is misleading. The only conclusion we can draw is that, despite the recent economic boom, poverty in India is still widespread and cuts across caste and religious barriers.

Education

The census measures literacy rates in terms of the percentage of persons 7 years and above who can read and write. Compared to a national average of 65.1 percent, Muslims register a modest 59 percent on the literacy scale with the SC/STs barely crossing the 50 percent mark. This marginal difference of 6 percent is not disastrous, a point which the report acknowledges by indicating that "the all-India literacy levels of Muslims are somewhat satisfactory."

While the 59 percent literacy rate of the Muslim is not deplorable, there is a small glitch in the education scene of the community: the quality and type of education imparted. By picking up on the 4 percent enrollment in *madrassas* (quoted by the Sachar Report) noted columnists have tended to counter the idea that Muslim education tends to be basically religious, parochial, exclusive, and not practical. This is a half-truth that is being deliberately disseminated and emphasized to win an ideological battle at the cost of ascertaining the true state of learning in that community.

Delving deeper into details, one unearths a picture that is definitely concerning. In addition to those attending *madrassas*, another 4 percent attend *maktabs*, religious schools affiliated with mosques. *Maktabs* by definition are meant to supplement mainstream education with a religious curriculum. The report avers that 60,000 students in Kerala attend both *maktabs* and regular schools. There is no information provided for other parts of the country.

The real issue, however, appears to be Urdu-medium schools. While the data presented are sketchy, what emerges is that a whopping 30–50 percent of Muslim students attend Urdu-medium schools in some states whose performance at the CBSE exam level falls short of national standards, bringing into question the very suitability of such schools to provide mainstream education apt for the modern changing world. Therein lies the crux of the problem.

Instead of obfuscating the issue by focusing on the 4 percent enrollment in *madrassas* and indulging in semantics, one needs to take an objective look at the overall inadequacy of education of Muslim students and suggest an appropriate solution: mainstream education for one and all.

A quota, while no doubt politically expedient, is not a panacea. With its myriad communities and religions, the politics of reservation can be suicidal for a country like India. Any solution must subscribe to these basic principles: equal opportunity for all, aid to the economically deprived regardless of caste or religion to ensure a level playing field, and emphasis on merit.

20

Hope and Reality

A few weeks ago, I read two articles ("Khan Saheb in Kashi"[1] by Shekhar Gupta* and "Treading Netherlands"[2] by Tavleen Singh**) in the same newspaper (*Indian Express*), both of which provided analytical perspectives of the Muslims in India from opposing viewpoints: one so poetic and lyrical that it touched the deepest chords in my heart imbuing in me an emotional and soothing euphoria in the process, one so graphically crafted that I could almost aurally sense the purity of Ustad Bismillah Khan's shehnai through the magic of those words; the other so harsh, critical and ostensibly crude at times that it jarred my eardrums with an overall effect that was cerebrally disturbing. One depicted India as the utopia that I dreamed of, the other showcased India as it actually was, warts and all. One was sweet music to my ears; the other hit me with the harsh reality that I wanted to escape.

In a superb exposé of literary talent Shekhar Gupta brilliantly captures the heartrending agony of India in the age of terrorism and sees a ray of hope in the likes of Ustad Bismillah Khan. Shekhar Gupta's Bismillah Khan is a rare human being, who, when he played *Rag Bhairavi*, blended the cultural ethos of *Bharatvarsha* into his beautiful persona finding no contradiction with his religion in the process. But is he the stereotype, or the exception? How I yearn to have a Muslim community more in his image (than the ungainly picture thrust upon

---

*   Editor, *Indian Express*.
**   Columnist, *Indian Express*.

them by present circumstances). And in reality the majority of them are, their true nature masked and suppressed by a vocally dominant fundamentalist clique. India has had no dearth of Muslim leaders who have distilled the culture of this ancient land through the spirit of their religion, Islam: Zakir Hussain, M. C. Chagla, Abul Kalam Azad, and our present president to name a few. Indian Muslims need to fashion themselves in the image of these individuals. These figures should be their role models. While this is the hope, is this the reality of today's India?

Tavleen Singh categorically refutes this optimism: "So from Kashmir to Kanyakumari these days you meet ordinary, '*nek, namazi*' Muslims who have started looking towards Arabia for their cultural roots. This is not just silly but sad because in doing this they are gradually forgetting the richness of our own culture and their immense contribution to it."

Shekhar Gupta is also right to aver: "No country can survive if it starts looking at nearly 15 per cent of its population as a fifth column." Nor should we. I fully concur with him when he asks rhetorically: "Can you profile 14 crore in a universe of a hundred crore?" But can we afford to overlook the fact that hidden among this 14 crores is a minuscule but committed fifth column that is not only bent on tarnishing the name of the community, but also intent on destroying the secular fabric of our nation?

Lost in this polemics of political correctness "we continue to be in denial about the transformation of ordinary, supposedly moderate Indian Muslims," Tavleen Singh rightly points out. She adds:

> … our Islamist problem will continue and grow unless we confront the truth that Indian Muslims have changed in recent years. Our political leaders and we of the ultra-liberal media refused to accept that we have an Islamist problem till the train bombers in Mumbai turned out to be Indian and not Pakistani. We have still not registered how serious the problem is or we would not have allowed the recent controversy over Vande Mataram. Muslim preachers like the rabid Imam of Delhi's Jama Masjid have used nationwide television to stir Muslims up against a song that is patriotic and not religious. The word "vande" does not necessarily

mean to pray, it can also mean to pay tribute, which is what the song does. After A. R. Rahman turned it into a wonderful, modern song, you would have thought that Muslim objections to singing it would have died, but they have not.

We can afford to ignore these disturbing trends only at our own peril.

Shekhar Gupta's conclusion embodies the aspiration of all Indians cutting across the great ideological divide: "If India can get this nuance right, it could be the toast of the world tomorrow for an even greater socio-political miracle, a secular but deeply religious nation that defeated terrorism while taking its 14 crore Muslims along."

We need to cling to this vision so beautifully expressed by Shekhar Gupta for that is what our land and culture is about: amalgamation. To loose that goal would be to loose ourselves, our true identity. However, there is a caveat: to get to that "promised land," we need to inculcate in ourselves the hard-nosed pragmatism that Tavleen Singh advocates.

21

India: The Need for a New Secularism

That we are having a perpetual debate on secularism is evidence enough that secularism, in India as we know it, has failed. The word "secular" pervades the political jargon in our country to suffocation and is bandied around in such reckless fashion that it has been reduced to nihilism: the obfuscation is total. No one really knows, no one really understands what it means and, above all, one sometimes feels that no one really cares. It has become little more than a political weapon to brand one's enemies. It is imperative that we redefine secularism in the Indian context clearly so that it is practically applicable and acceptable to all sections of our society, as a genuine guiding force that will be able to maintain a harmonious balance between India's myriad castes and communities and nurture an environment that is fair to one and all.

The evolution of the concept of secularism in the West compared to that in India is quite distinct. In the West, the Church with its rigid parochial outlook had definite political ambitions with a tendency to interfere in all facets of human life, personal, communal, and scientific. The public showdown between Galileo and the Church is a classic example of this intrusion, so is the opposition to Darwin's theory of evolution. This proved to be detrimental to the welfare of the State and to human progress. The Church had no place for non-believers. Heretics, religious or scientific, were ostracized or coerced into submission. Enlightened individuals recognized this deleterious influence of religion and sought to minimize it by an enforced separation of Church and State.

In contrast, the spiritual influence in India for ages was Hinduism, more a way of life than a formalized religion. Enshrined in its teachings were the key tenets of *Vasudaiva Kutumbakkam* (The World is One) and *Ekam Sat Viprah Bahuda Vadaiti* (Truth is One; the Wise Call it by Different Names). This philosophy is an inherent part of our thinking, has been woven into the fabric of our society, and is a defining trait of our identity. The refuge provided to and acceptance of diverse persecuted communities like Parsees, Jews, and Tibetans into our fold clearly reflects this. Religious *acceptance*, not merely religious *tolerance*, describes our society more aptly. The term religious tolerance has a negative connotation. Religious tolerance is fitting for those societies that do not accept the validity of other religions.

Moreover, Hinduism with its matrix structure and lack of central authority never posed a threat to the political establishment. Therefore, this enforced separation of religion and State was not a necessity unlike as in the West.

And so, for ages, we lived in this world of ours guided rightly by these principles but naively believing that the world outside and people of different cultures too subscribed to our world vision. We were rudely jolted out of this peaceful slumber when a "clash of civilizations" occurred, in the form of an intolerant, marauding Muslim invasion and an expansionist Christian British colonialism. Herein lie the seeds of the failure of our modern secularism; our inability to handle the changing demographics that these events forced on us; our inability to effectively confront these differing ideologies that had found their way into our midst.

When India finally broke free of the shackles of foreign subjugation in 1947 and a new state came into existence, we naturally and rightly reaffirmed our commitment to secularism, which had always been our tradition. But there were challenges ahead. The vivisection of India and the creation of a fanatically Islamic Pakistan had awakened a new assertiveness in the Hindu. The Muslims who remained in India feared domination by an overwhelming Hindu population. What should have been tackled with intellectual foresight, truth, and justice was affected by a simplistic, self-flagellating and sometimes deceitful approach that placed the entire onus on the Hindu.

Fearing that Hindu resurgence would be along the lines of Nazi Germany, every attempt was made to suppress the Hindu identity; secularism in post-modern India was equated, to all intents and purposes, with negation of the Hindu identity. The methodology that was adopted was bizarre and warped. History was rewritten to show that the dark period of Islamic invasion was in reality a golden period. Hindus were told that their temples were never destroyed, their people never coerced or lured into accepting other religions. Whatever had happened was due to their own weaknesses and the ills that plagued Hindu society. Anyone attempting to oppose this line of thought was branded a communalist and summarily suppressed. Moreover, this new-fangled ideology led to showering on the non-Hindu communities a set of privileges that could not be justified morally, economically, or legally.

I agree this was a philosophy that was well-intentioned, but the manner in which it was implemented through a combination of deceit, manipulation, and inequality (strong words, true nevertheless) was certainly questionable. It was bound to fail and it did.

Now we need to reformulate these principles taking into account the ground realities. We need to confront our past honestly and with courage. We need to understand each other and remove the distrust. We need to respect each other. We need to ensure that every Indian be judged on his own merit regardless of religion, caste, creed, or sex.

A candid appreciation of our history is a must, warts and all. Trust cannot be built on a foundation of lies. Neither can we wish away the ills of the past. Much as we deny it, much as we may not like it, history casts a long shadow on the present with the capability to disrupt the future. I feel that all communities in India have the strength to face their past with maturity and dignity.

Once we get over this initial hurdle, we can formulate a sound philosophy that will succeed and should be one of *shared responsibility*. I envision the following as the three pillars of a new secularism:

1) Religious détente;

2) Demographic status quo; and

3) Equality for all.

Religious Détente

Principle: *Respect for each others' religions.*

Dr S. Radhakrishnan, noted philosopher and the first vice-president of India, made this observation about Indian secularism.

> It may appear somewhat strange that our Government should be a secular one while our culture is rooted in spiritual values. Secularism here does not mean irreligious[ness] or atheism or even stress on material comforts. It proclaims that it lays stress on the universalisation of spiritual values which may be attained by a variety of ways.[1]

Note the emphasis on "… the universalisation of spiritual values which may be attained by a *variety of ways*" (italics mine). Mutual respect for each other's religion is vital in a pluralistic society. However, the intrinsic ideological variation among the major religions in India makes this task formidable, almost to the point of impossibility. A question often asked is how Hinduism can reconcile with a religion (Christianity) whose avowed principle is conversion and another (Islam) which swears by the motto, convert, or get exterminated? The chasm appears too wide. This is not a perception of the RSS or the VHP alone as many in India would like us to believe. Octavia Paz, the Nobel Prize–winning Mexican writer who spent several years in India as the Mexican ambassador had this to say about Islam in his *Light of India*:

> Between Islam and Hinduism there is not only an opposition, but an incompatibility.… The separation had existed since the founding of the Delhi Sultanate in 1206. With the exception of Akbar, none of the Muslim rulers, for seven centuries, made any real attempt to transform coexistence into a genuine

reconciliation. Their religion would not allow it: idolaters must be either converted or exterminated.[2]

Sri Aurobindo, one of India's greatest seers, was greatly disturbed by this inherent bigotry and posed this question about Islam: "You can live with a religion whose principle is toleration. But how is it possible to live with a religion whose principle is 'I will not tolerate you'? How are you going to have unity with these people?"[3] So what do we do now? How does India as a nation address this issue? How can India maintain the delicate balance between its myriad religious communities and continue its long tradition of religious acceptance? How can we reconcile these irreconcilable differences? A religious détente is necessary.

The world is changing, respect for each other's opinion is now the norm, and the plurality of religions in our region makes it imperative to follow this: it is essential for peaceful coexistence. While Hinduism has never claimed exclusive divine sanction, other religions are still not willing give up this rigid stance. Some Christian priests in the subcontinent (probably because of Hinduism's overwhelming influence and their knowledge of other religions) do accept the Hindu principle of *Ekam Sat Viprah Bahuda Vadait* (Truth is One).

Father Tissa Balasuriya, a Sri Lankan priest and scholar, argued that "… the Roman Catholic Church and Christianity in general must go farther to acknowledge the legitimacy of other faiths" (*New York Times*, April 24, 2005). For this, he was excommunicated from the Church, with which he eventually reconciled. Nevertheless, this signifies a ray of hope.

Conversion is another area of concern and strikes at the very concept of "the legitimacy of other faiths." When one accepts the validity of another religion, conversion becomes a moot point. Zealous conversion must be prohibited; better, if the Christians and Muslims of India voluntarily give up all proselytization and proscribe terms like "heathen" and "kafir" from their religious books. Is that too much to ask? Aggressive proselytization can only serve to disturb the religious ecology and create discord between people. Conversion is the raison d'être for the distrust between religions. In the absence of this cantankerous issue, religions will be able to coexist peacefully.

Religions like Islam and Christianity must not view these changes as a compromise but as an evolutionary step in keeping with the times and as a positive contribution to the growth and sustenance of secularism in India.

Demographic Status Quo

Principle: *Each religion must give up practices that are directly harmful or against the interests of another.*

Due to differing birth control practices the demography of India is changing, with the Hindu population growing at a much slower rate than other communities. Despite the fact that the present government tinkered with the figures of the present census (after they were published) to project a different picture, one cannot deny the reality. Fear and anxiety about numerical domination can be put to rest if a common birth control policy is adopted, equally applied to all communities. Birth control is not an option but a necessity. India's burgeoning population needs to be brought under control to avoid a catastrophe and all communities need to contribute to this.

Equality

Principle: *Every citizen and every religion must be treated as equal by law.*

Equality must be the cornerstone of this secular policy. Every individual and every religion must be treated equally. Donald E. Smith, Professor of Political Science in Pennsylvania University, provides this working definition of a secular state. "The secular State is a State which guarantees individual and corporate freedom of religion, deals with the individual as a citizen irrespective of his religion, is not constitutionally connected to a particular religion, nor does it seek to promote or interfere with religion."[4] This definition must be applied to the letter.

The state must view every individual as a person irrespective of his religion or caste or sex. In such an environment there can be no minority or majority. Privileges should be conferred on need-based criteria. And a common law applicable to all Indians must be introduced. The Supreme Court of India concurs with this policy stating that labels like "minority" promote fragmentation of society and encourage fissiparous tendencies:

> Differential treatments to linguistic minorities based on language within the state is understandable but if the same concept for minorities on the basis of religion is encouraged, the whole country, which is already under class and social conflicts due to various divisive forces, will further face division on the basis of religious diversities. Such claims to minority status based on religion would increase in the fond hope of various sections of people getting special protections, privileges and treatment as part of constitutional guarantee. Encouragement to such fissiparous tendencies would be a serious jolt to the secular structure of constitutional democracy. We should guard against making our country akin to a theocratic state based on multi-nationalism. Our concept of secularism, to put it in a nut shell, is that the 'state' will have no religion. The state will treat all religions and religious groups equally and with equal respect without in any manner interfering with their individual rights of religion, faith and worship.[5]

Under our present system, all religions are not treated equally; Hinduism bears an unfair share of the burden. While churches and mosques enjoy freedom from government control, Hindu temples, to a large extent, continue to be administered by the government, a system that engenders corrupt practices, misuse of funds, and an unjust siphoning off of revenues generated by Hindu temples to support non-Hindu establishments.

These figures from the Karnataka Government are a classic example of how Hindu funds have been unfairly diverted to promote Christian and Muslim establishments (Sandhya Jain, Robbing Peter to pay Paul-The Karnataka Way, *Daily Pioneer*, May 12, 2005).

In 2000, temples generated revenues of Rs. 69.96 crore,* but received only Rs. 13.75 crore for maintenance. The *madrassa*–hajj subsidy was gifted Rs. 35 crore. In 2002, the state received Rs. 72 crore as revenue, returned Rs. 10 crore for temple maintenance, and granted Rs. 50 crore for *madrassas* and Rs. 10 crore for churches.

Subsidy for hajj pilgrimage has been another bone of contention for a long time. With such blatant interference in the affairs of a particular religion and uninhibited promotion of others, how can we call ourselves a secular state? Is this not a violation of basic secular tenets? Does this not create bitterness rather than communal amity? The state must refrain from all interference in the affairs of any religion and only ensure that one does not violate the rights of another.

With these goals in mind I am confident that we can usher in a just society that will bring peace and prosperity to all Indians.

---

*   1 crore equals 10 million.

22

Note of Caution

The zeal of *Hindutva* has to be tempered with good sense and good judgment taking into account the ground reality. Hinduism has always been a system that places a premium on individual freedom and acceptance of other religions. In order for *Hindutva* to be successful, it cannot be restrictive in its outlook or take on a rigid conservative garb. It should be a force that is not afraid to admit and rectify the traditional ills that afflict Indian society. A backward, poverty-stricken, inward-looking country is not what *Hindutva* aims to shape India into. Harmless celebrations like Valentine's Day should not be frowned upon and imposition of a dress code (like the Taliban in Afghanistan and Islamic extremists in Kashmir) should not be enforced. By focusing on these insignificant issues, we stand to alienate a significant portion of the population and thus jeopardize the ultimate goal.

Without proper guidance, there is a real danger of *Hindutva* degenerating into a rampage of revenge. *Hindutva* is not to be equated with communal riots that kill innocent humans. *Hindutva* cannot be an ideology that relegates another individual to second-class status. It should be a force that makes all Indians conform to the pluralistic, secular tradition of our land that respects one and all.

In other words, Hindutva should always evoke the image of Sri Ram: strong and powerful, yet humane and compassionate.

Glossary

Political Parties:	Bharatiya Janata Party (BJP)
	Indian National Congress
	Communist Party of India–Marxist (CPM)
	Communist Party of India (CPI)

National Democratic Alliance (NDA): A coalition of political parties headed by the BJP which ruled India from 1996 to 2004.

United Progressive Alliance (UPA): A coalition of parties led by the Indian National Congress, opposed to the BJP.

Rashtriya Swayamsevak Sangh (RSS): A voluntary socio-cultural organization founded in 1925, at the fag end of the British rule, with the specific aim of instilling a sense of confidence and patriotism among Indians, who had until then suffered foreign domination for nearly a thousand years. It emphasizes India's Hindu civilization and has multiple sister organizations involved in active social work. Has strong links with the BJP.

Sangh Parivar (Sangh Family): Also known as the saffron (the traditional color of Hindus) brigade, a term used to refer to the various organizations that are loosely connected with and subscribe to the concept of Hindu/Indian Nationalism.

Major print media: *The Indian Express*
Hindustan Times
The Times of India
The Hindu
Daily Pioneer
Deccan Herald
Outlook (weekly newsmagazine)
Frontline (weekly newsmagazine)

Pseudo-secularism:	A warped idea of secularism espoused by a section of Indians (especially the English-language media as opposed to the vernacular press), which in reality amounts to Hindu-bashing.
Sikh Riots:	Occurred in late 1984, in reaction to the assassination of Prime Minister Indira Gandhi of the Congress Party by her two Sikh bodyguards, in which thousands of Sikhs were killed by a politically instigated mob.
Nanavati Commission:	A government inquiry into the anti-Sikh Riots.
Chief Minister:	Equivalent to Governor in the United States.
Hurriyat:	Confederation of Kashmiri organizations fighting for greater autonomy.
Puranas:	Ancient Hindu scriptures.
Vedas:	Ancient Hindu scriptures.
Gujarat 2002:	Refers to the Hindu-Muslim riots that rocked Gujarat in March 2002 in the aftermath of the gruesome killing of 59 Hindus by a Muslim mob in the town of Godhra in Gujarat.

Notes and References

Chapter 1. Introduction

1. Walia CJS. *Indiastar Review of Books Online*. http;//www.indiastar. com.

   Danielou, Alan. *Histôire de l'Inde* (French). Fayard, 1983.

2. Durant, Will. *The Story of Civilization*. New York: Simon and Schuster, 1954, p. 459.

3. Gautier, Francois. *Rewriting Indian History*. New Delhi: India Research Press, 2003.

4. Savarkar, V. D. *Hindutva*. New Delhi: Hindi Sahitya Sadan, 2003.

5. Supreme Court of India, *Manohar Joshi vs Nitin Bhaurao Patil*, 1995, 8: 646.

6. Hariharan, Githa. April 4, 2004. "Our Forgettable Forefathers." *Telegraph*.

7. Mishra, Balram. January 23, 2007. "Notional Crisis." *Hindustan Times*:

   After becoming a Sarsanghchalak (leader), Golwalkar distanced himself from the views expressed in *We, or Our Nationhood Defined*. This has been elaborated by the historian, Devendra Swarup, in an essay published in the weekly, *Panchajanya*, on February 17, 1980. The write-up is based on an interview the author had with Golwalkar in 1962 at Prayag. The interviewer asked Golwalkar, "Country, race, language, religion and culture are said to be the five syndromes of a nation. If all these elements are found together in their full bloom, shall we say that nationhood has been attained?" Golwalkar shot back, "[This] concept of nationhood...belonged to the 19th century. Now it is obsolete. It is not necessary that all these five elements be available together at a given point of time to indicate the group consciousness of nationalism."

Swarup asked, "Doesn't your book…interpret nationalism on the basis of these five elements?" Golwalkar replied, "Forget about that book. It is outdated."

8.   Sen, Amartya. *The Argumentative Indian*. New York: Picador, 2005, pp. 53, 72.

Chapter 2. Naipaul's India: "The Hindu Land is a Wounded Civilization"

1.   Naipaul, V. S. *An Area of Darkness*. New York: Vintage Books, 1964.

2.   Naipaul, V. S. *A Wounded Civilization*. New York: Vintage Books, 1977.

3.   Naipaul, V. S. *India: A Million Mutinies Now*. New York: Viking, 1991.

4.   Paine, Jeffery. *Father India*. New York: Harper Collins, 1998.

Chapter 3. India as an Entity.

1.   Nehru, Jawaharlal. *Glimpses of World History*. Oxford University Press, 1982.

2.   Jain, Girilal. *A Hindu Phenomenon*. New Delhi: UBSPD, 1994.

3.   Keay, John. *India: A History*. New York: Atlantic Monthly Press, 2000.

Other notes:

a)   Map 2: India during the Mauryan Empire (250 B.C.), source: *Wikipedia*

b)   Map 4: Europe in A.D. 1, source: ©2003, C. Nussli, www.euratlas.com

c)   Map 5: British India, source: *Wikipedia*.

Chapter 4. Controversy about History

1.   Keay, John. *India: A History*. New York: Atlantic Press, 2000.

2.   Feuerstein, George, Subhash Kak and David Frawley. *In Search of the Cradle of Civilization*. Wheaton, Illinois: Quest Books, 1995.

3.   Danino, Michael. *The Invasion that Never Was*. Mysore, India: Mother's Institute of Research & Mira Aditi, 1996.

4.   Shourie, Arun, Harsh Narain, Jay Dubashi, Ram Swarup and Sita Ram Goel. *Hindu Temples: What Happened to Them*. New Delhi: Voice of India Publications, 1990.

5.   Shourie, Arun. *Eminent Historians: Their Technology, Their Line, Their Fraud*. Harper Collins, 1999.

6.   Srinivasan, Rajeev. January 4, 2002. "Indians Will No Longer be Impressed with Marxist Histrionics," *Rediff*.

7.   Muralidharan, Sivakumar. January 19, 2002. "The History Congress Session." *Frontline*.

Chapter 5. Truth in History: Destruction of Hindu Temples

1.   Eaton, Richard. December 9, 2000. "Temple Desecration in Pre-Modern India." *Frontline*.

2.   Singh, Khushwant. *We Indians*. New Delhi: Orient Paperback, 1982.

Chapter 6. Changing Demography of South Asia

1.   Hindu American Foundation. "Hindus in Bangladesh, Pakistan and Kashmir: A Survey of Human Rights 2004." Kensington, MD: Hindu American Foundation, 2004.

2.   Census of India, *Census of India Online*, http://www.censusindia.net

3.   Sinha, Lt. Gen. S. K. November 8, 1998. "Illegal Migration into Assam." Report submitted to the President of India.

4.   Griswold, Eliza. January 23, 2005. "The Next Islamist Revolution?" *New York Times*.

Chapter 8. Kashmiri Pandits: Ethnic Cleansing the World does not see.

1. *The systematic manner in which the Sikhs were thus killed indicate that the attacks on them were organized.*

    Whatever acts were done, were done by the local Congress (I) leaders and workers, and they appear to have done so for their personal political reasons. If they were the acts of individuals only, then the killing of Sikhs and looting of properties of Sikhs would not have been on such a large scale. Therefore, what those local leaders appear to have done is to take help of their followers and supporters in inciting or committing those acts: Nanavati Report, Part iv.

2. Internal Displacement Monitoring Center, *IDMC Online*, http://www. internal-displacement.org, February 24, 2007.

3. Gupta, Kanchan. January 19, 2005. "19/01/90: When Kashmiri Pandits Fled Islamic Terror." *Rediff.*

4. Amnesty International, *Amnesty International Online*, http://www. amnesty.org

Chapter 9. Amarnath: A Lesson in Secularism

1. Swami, Praveen. August 17, 2002. "A Troubled Trek." *Frontline.*

Chapter 11. Lies, lies and More Lies.

1. Gautier, Francois. February 1, 1999. "A Warped Indian Media?" *Hindustan Times.*

2. Roy, Arundhati. May 6, 2002. "Who's She When She's at Home?" *Outlook India.*

3. May 27, 2002. *Outlook India.*

4. Punj, Balbir. July 8, 2002. "Dissimulation in Words and in Images." *Outlook India.*

5. Vardarajan, Tunku. January 11, 1999. "Deadly Zeal in India." *New York Times.*

Chapter 14. Godhra and its Aftermath

1.   "Gujarat Carnage 2002. A Report to the Nation—An Independent Fact-Finding Mission." *Outlook/Web.* April 11, 2002.

2.   *The Commission also agrees with the findings recorded by Justice Mishra Commission as regards the delay in calling the army*: Nanavati Report, part iv.

3.   Ramdas, L. March 11, 2002. "An Open Letter to the PM." *Outlook.*

4.   Sethi, Harsh. March 16, 2002. "Frayed at the Edges." *The Hindu.*

5.   Jha, Prem Shankar. April 22, 2002. "Gujarat: A Sober Diary." *Outlook.*

Chapter 15. Hindu Temples in the Age of Pseudo-Secularism

1.   September 9, 2006. "HC Strikes Down Act on Temples." *Deccan Herald.*

2.   Patel, Anjali. "Revenues from Temples Diverted for Haj Subsidy and Madarassas in Karnataka." *IVarta.com.* Source: Revenue Section, Tourism and Temples, Government of Karnataka.

Chapter 16. Indian Intellectuals: A Failure to Lead

1.   Jaleel, Muzamil. July 22, 2006. "Reality Hits Home." *Indian Express.*

2.   Fernandes, Naresh. July 22, 2006. "India's Indestructible Heart." *New York Times.* July 12, 2006.

3.   Kulkarni, Sudheendra. July 14, 2006. "Keeping Peace: Will the Spirit of Bombay Rise to the Challenge?" *Indian Express.*

Chapter 18. Freedom of Religion and Conversion Not Synonymous

1.   *Collected Works of Mahatma Gandhi*, vol. 28, p. 57; vol. 67, p. 48; vol. 70, p. 244.

Chapter 19. The Sachar Report

1.   Gautier, Francois. May 23, 2006. "Are Brahmins the Dalits of Today."
      Rediff.

Chapter 20. Hope and Reality

1.   Gupta, Shekhar. August 26, 2006. "Khan Saheb in Kasi." *Indian
      Express.*

2.   Singh, Tavleen. August 27, 2006. "Treading Netherlands." *Indian
      Express.*

Chapter 21. India: The Need for a New Secularism

1.   Radhakrishnan, S. Foreword in Abid Hussain, *National Culture of India.*
      New Delhi: National Book Trust, 1956.

2.   Paz, Octavia. *In Light of India.* Harvest Books, 1998.

3.   Sri Aurobindo. *India's Rebirth.* Mysore, India: Mira Aditi Center, Part
      III, p. 2.

4.   Smith, Donald Eugene. *India as a Secular State.* Princeton: Princeton
      University Press, 1967.

5.   Supreme Court of India Judgment, August 8, 2005. *Bal Patil vs Union
      of India.* Case No. 4730, 1999.

978-0-595-43549-4
0-595-43549-1